# Praise for *Palestine Peace Not Apartheid*

"The former president's ideas are expressed with perfect clarity; his book, of course, represents a personal point of view, but one that is certainly grounded in both knowledge and wisdom. His outlook on the problem not only contributes to the literature of debate surrounding it but also, just as importantly, delivers a worthy game plan for clearing up the dilemma."

—*Booklist*

"Thirty years after his first trip to the Mideast, former President Jimmy Carter still has hope for a peaceful, comprehensive solution to the region's troubles, delivering this informed and readable chronicle as an offering to the cause. . . . Carter's book provides a fine overview for those unfamiliar with the history of the conflict and lays out an internationally accepted blueprint for peace."

—*Publishers Weekly*

"Part history, part memoir, part roadmap, *Palestine Peace Not Apartheid* takes the debate about the constant crisis in the Middle East beyond clichés and talking points. Carter does not pull punches. He says what must be done—and, in large part, he is speaking to the American people, who must force their elected leaders to make this country an honest player in a region where U.S. actions have fostered far more grief than hope."

—John Nichols, *The Capital Times* (Madison, Wisconsin)

"Carter . . . has provoked a much-needed discussion that rarely ever transpires in U.S. politics and media."

—Sherri Muzher, *The Detroit News*

"A good, strong read by the only American president approaching sainthood . . . An honourable, honest account by a friend of Israel as well as the Arabs who just happens to be a fine American ex-statesman."

—Robert Fisk, *The Sunday Tribune* (Ireland)

"An important new book."

—Gary Kamiya, Salon.com

"Makes for compelling reading . . . provides an important reminder that the Camp David agreement not only created a durable peace between Egypt and Israel but served as a model for all of the major Israeli-Palestinian peace initiatives that were to follow."

—Henry Siegman, *The Nation*

"If there is a contemporary figure who can offer a credible solution to the crisis [in the Middle East], it is former President Jimmy Carter. . . . Carter has an innate understanding of the Middle East and its complexities. . . . He offers timely thoughts on how to restore peace to the region."

—John T. Slania, *Bookpage*

ALSO BY JIMMY CARTER

# JIMMY
# CARTER

# PALESTINE PEACE NOT APARTHEID

—— •◆• ——

SIMON & SCHUSTER PAPERBACKS

New York London Toronto Sydney

SIMON & SCHUSTER PAPERBACKS
1230 Avenue of the Americas
New York, NY 10020

Copyright © 2006 by Jimmy Carter
Afterword copyright © 2007 by Jimmy Carter

First Simon & Schuster trade paperback edition September 2007

SIMON & SCHUSTER PAPERBACKS and colophon are registered trademarks of Simon & Schuster, Inc.

For information about special discounts for bulk purchases, please contact Simon & Schuster Special Sales at 1-800-456-6798 or business@simonandschuster.com.

Designed by C. Linda Dingler
Maps by Paul J. Pugliese

Manufactured in the United States of America

1   3   5   7   9   10   8   6   4   2

Library of Congress Cataloging-in-Publication Data

Carter, Jimmy.
Palestine peace not apartheid / Jimmy Carter.
p. cm.
Includes index.
1. Arab-Israeli conflict—1973–1993. 2. Arab-Israeli conflict—1993—Peace. 3. United States—Foreign relations—Middle East. 4. Middle East—Foreign relations—United States. 5. Israel—Politics and government—1973–1993. 6. Israel—Politics and government—1993– 7. Palestinian Arabs—Politics and government—1973–1993. 8. Palestinian Arabs—Politics and government—1993–.
9. United States President (1977–1981 : Carter). I. Title.
DS119.7.C3583 2006
956.04—dc22
2006050997

ISBN-13: 978-0-7432-8502-5
ISBN-10:    0-7432-8502-6
ISBN-13: 978-0-7432-8503-2 (PBK)
ISBN-10:    0-7432-8503-4 (PBK)

To our first great-grandchild, Henry Lewis Carter,
with hopes that he will see peace
and justice in the Holy Land

————•◆•————

# CONTENTS

——— •◆• ———

*ix*

# LIST OF MAPS

———•◆•———

# Map 1

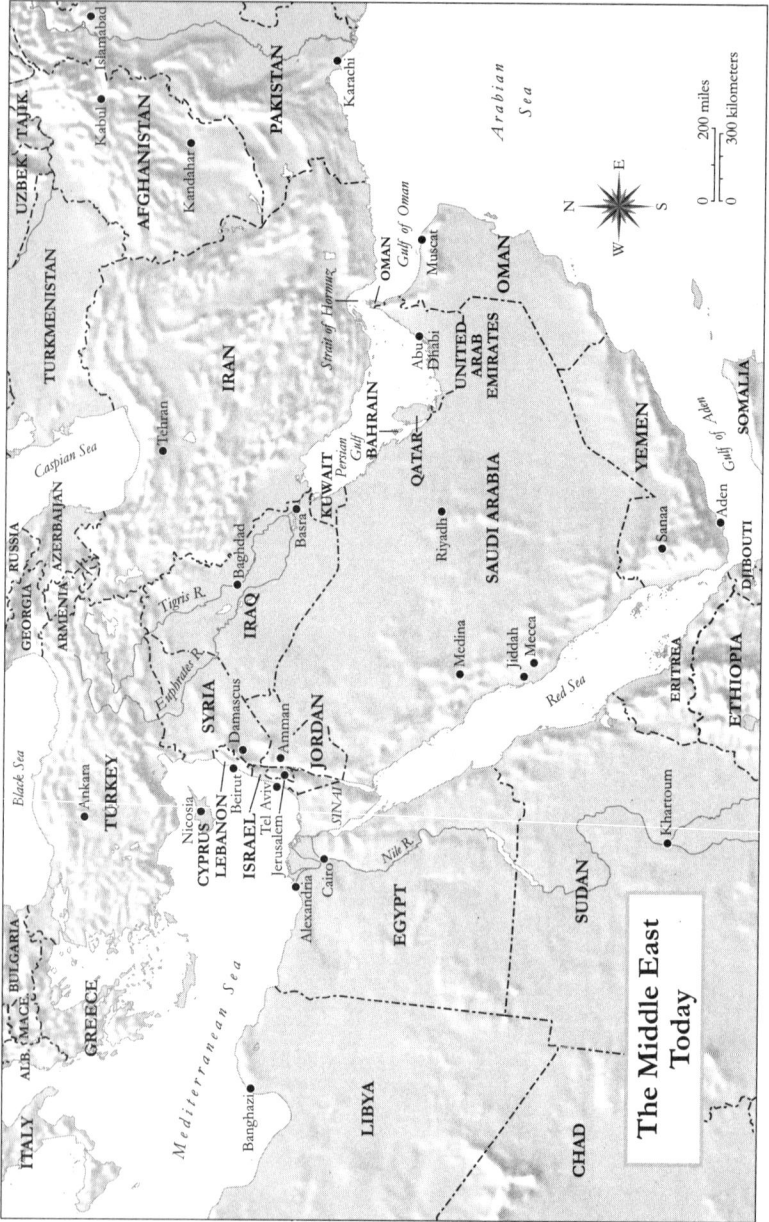

The Middle East Today

# Map 2

# Map 3

**Israel 1949–67**

Damascus ★
LEBANON  •Mt. Hermon

Tyre •

SYRIA

Zefat •

Haifa •

Sea of Galilee

Nazareth •

•Irbid

*Mediterranean Sea*

Jenin •

Netanya •

•Nablus

Jordan River

Tel Aviv •

Ramallah •

★Amman

JORDAN

Jerusalem ★

N
W    E
S

Gaza •

Hebron •

Dead Sea

Gaza Strip
(Egyptian
Administration)  •Rafah

•Beersheba

•Al Karak

•El Arish

ISRAEL

*NEGEV*

EGYPT

*SINAI*

| 0 | 10 | 20 | 30 miles |
| 0 | 10 20 30 | 40 kilometers |

– – – – –  U.N. Approved
Boundary

Eilat •
•Aqaba

Gulf of
Aqaba

SAUDI
ARABIA

*The Bible says that when the first blood was shed among His children, God asked Cain, the slayer, "Where is Abel thy brother?" And he said, "I know not. Am I my brother's keeper?" And the Lord said, "What hast thou done? The voice of thy brother's blood crieth unto me from the ground. And now art thou cursed . . ."*

(GENESIS 4:9–11)

*The blood of Abraham, God's father of the chosen, still flows in the veins of Arab, Jew, and Christian, and too much of it has been spilled in grasping for the inheritance of the revered patriarch in the Middle East. The spilled blood in the Holy Land still cries out to God—an anguished cry for peace.*

—from *The Blood of Abraham*, by Jimmy Carter

# HISTORICAL CHRONOLOGY

————— • ◆ • —————

Developments in the Middle East can best be understood if the history of the region is reviewed. Listed here are a few of the important events that have led to the existing state of affairs.

ca. 1900 B.C.: Abraham journeys from Ur to Canaan.

ca. 1200 B.C.: Moses leads the Israelites' exodus from Egypt.

ca. 1000 B.C.: King David unites the twelve tribes of Israel, then his son Solomon builds the Temple in Jerusalem.

ca. 930 B.C.: The Israelite nation divides into two weaker kingdoms, Israel and Judah. Israel is conquered by the Assyrians about 720 B.C., and Judah is destroyed by the Babylonians in 586 B.C.

ca. 538 B.C.: Persia conquers Babylon and permits exiled Jews to return to Jerusalem.

332 B.C.: Greeks conquer the region.

167 B.C.: Jews establish an independent Judaea.

63 B.C.: Romans establish control over Judaea.

ca. 4 B.C.: Jesus is born. He is crucified thirty-three years later after a ministry of three years. Christian churches are established throughout the eastern Roman Empire.

A.D. 70: A Jewish revolt against Rome is put down and the Temple is destroyed.

135: Romans suppress a Jewish revolt, killing or forcing almost all Jews of Judaea into exile. The Romans name the province Syria Palaestina.

ca. 325: The Roman Emperor Constantine, a Christian, strengthens his own religion throughout the region.

ca. 570: The Prophet Muhammad is born in Mecca, establishes the Islamic faith, unites the Arabian Peninsula, and dies in 632. Arabic rule and faith spread rapidly throughout Syria Palaestina, Persia, and Egypt.

1099: The first Crusaders capture Jerusalem and establish Christian rule over Palestine.

1187: Saladin, sultan of Egypt, conquers Jerusalem and, except for a fifteen-year interval, Muslims control Palestine until the end of World War I.

1516: The Ottoman Turks take Syria, Palestine, and then Egypt.

1861: The French establish Lebanon as an autonomous district within Syria, under Christian leadership.

1882: British forces occupy Egypt and remain there until 1955.

1917: Great Britain, during World War I, issues the Balfour Declaration, promising a Jewish national home in Palestine, with respect for the rights of non-Jewish Palestinians.

1922: After the Ottoman Empire is defeated in World War I, the League of Nations confirms British mandates over Iraq and Palestine, and a French mandate over Syria and Lebanon. Transjordan is separated from the Palestine Mandate and becomes an autonomous kingdom.

1936: Palestinian Arabs demand a halt to Jewish immigration and a ban on land sales to Jews. British troops attempt to assert control, but violence continues. The Peel Commission recommends partition of Palestine between Arabs and Jews.

1939: Britain announces severe restrictions on Jewish immigration and land purchases in Palestine. Violence erupts from Jewish militants.

1947: Britain lets the United Nations decide what to do about Palestine, which is partitioned into Jewish, Arab, and international areas (Jerusalem and Bethlehem). Fifty-five percent of the territory is allocated to the Jewish state. Egypt, Syria, Lebanon, and Jordan are now independent states.

1948: The British mandate over Palestine terminates. Israelis declare their independence as a nation, Arab armies attack, and Israel prevails. U.N. General Assembly Resolution 194 establishes a conciliation commission and asserts that refugees wishing to return to their homes and live at peace should be allowed to do so, that compensation should be paid to others, and that free access to the holy places should be assured.

1949: Armistice agreements with the Arabs allow Israel to gain more land (77 percent of Palestine). Egypt occupies the Gaza Strip. Transjordan, renamed Jordan, controls what is left of the west bank of the Jordan River, including Old Jerusalem, and in 1950 annexes this territory.

1956:  Egypt nationalizes the Suez Canal, and Israel
joins Britain and France in occupying the canal
area. Under international pressure all foreign
forces withdraw from Egyptian territories by the
next year. U.N. forces are assigned to patrol
strategic areas of the Sinai.

1964:  The Palestine Liberation Organization (PLO) is
established, committed to wage a battle to liberate
the homeland of the Palestinian people.

1967:  Egypt blockades the Straits of Tiran, and Arab
forces make menacing moves. Israel launches
preemptive attacks on Egypt, Syria, Iraq, and then
Jordan, and within six days occupies the Golan
Heights, Gaza, the Sinai, and the West Bank,
including Jerusalem.

Six months later, U.N. Security Council Resolution
242 is passed, confirming the inadmissibility of the
acquisition of land by force and calling for Israel's
withdrawal from occupied territories, the right of all
states in the region to live in peace within secure and
recognized borders, and a just solution to the refugee
problem.

1973:  Egypt and Syria attack Israeli forces in the Sinai and
Golan Heights. This conflict becomes known as the

Yom Kippur War. After sixteen days of war, U.N. Resolution 338 is passed, confirming Resolution 242 and calling for international peace talks. Various disengagement agreements follow.

1974: The Arab summit at Rabat in Morocco unanimously proclaims the PLO as the sole legitimate representative of the Palestinian people. Israel agrees to withdraw from Syrian territory, except for control of the Golan Heights.

1975: Civil war erupts in Lebanon. With approval from the international community the following year, Syria sends troops to establish order.

1977: Egyptian President Anwar al-Sadat visits Jerusalem and outlines Arab demands to the Israeli Knesset. Israeli Prime Minister Menachem Begin makes a return visit to Ismailia, with no progress toward peace.

1978: The Camp David Accords are approved by Israel and Egypt, confirming Israel's compliance with U.N. Resolution 242, withdrawal of political and military forces from the West Bank and Gaza, and full autonomy for Palestinians. The Accords outline a peace agreement between Israel and Egypt and other Arab neighbors. The Accords are rejected by the Arabs at the Baghdad summit, and Egypt is isolated.

1979:  A peace treaty is signed between Israel and Egypt, guaranteeing withdrawal of Israel from the Sinai, normal diplomatic relations, and Israel's access to the Suez Canal.

1981:  Israel escalates establishment of settlements on Palestinian territory. Egyptian President Anwar al-Sadat is assassinated.

1982:  In response to terrorist attacks across Lebanon's border, Israeli troops move into Lebanon, seeking to destroy PLO forces there. The militant Lebanese organization known as Hezbollah is established. Subsequent actions by the Israelis in Lebanon draw international criticism.

1985:  Israel partially removes its forces from Lebanon.

1987:  A Palestinian *intifada* (uprising) erupts, and Israel responds to the violence with harsh reprisals. The militant Palestinian organization known as Hamas is established.

1988:  Jordan cedes its rights in the West Bank and East Jerusalem to the PLO. PLO head Yasir Arafat acknowledges Israel's right to exist and renounces violence. The U.S. and the PLO initiate dialogue.

1991:  The Persian Gulf War ejects Iraqi forces that have invaded Kuwait. Many Palestinian exiles move to

Jordan. A Middle East peace conference, focusing on Arab-Israeli relations, is convened in Madrid.

1993: Israel and the PLO conclude a peace agreement in Oslo with mutual recognition and a five-year plan to resolve all remaining differences. Militant Palestinians and right-wing Israelis begin attempts to undermine the agreement.

1994: The Palestinian National Authority is established. Israel and Jordan sign a comprehensive peace agreement.

1995: Israeli Prime Minister Yitzhak Rabin is assassinated by an Israeli right-wing religious fanatic. This setback to the peace process is exacerbated by violent attacks from Palestinian groups opposed to the Oslo Agreement.

1996: Palestinians elect Yasir Arafat as president and elect the members of a legislative council. Israelis return the Likud Party to power, which stalls the Oslo process.

1998: The Wye River Memorandum is issued after talks between the Israelis and the Palestinians, under U.S. auspices. An airport is opened in Gaza, with flights to Arab nations.

2000: Israeli forces are withdrawn from Lebanon except for a disputed area, Shebaa Farms. Peace

negotiations at Camp David break down. Ariel
Sharon visits the Temple Mount and a second
intifada is launched, more violent than the first.

2001: Ariel Sharon is elected prime minister of Israel,
committed to rejection of the Oslo peace agreement
and an emphasis on national security. The Gaza
airport runway is bulldozed.

2002: An Arab League summit meeting endorses a Saudi
peace plan based on U.N. Resolutions 242 and 338.
Suicide bombings provoke strong Israeli response.
Sharon blames Arafat for the violence and confines
him in his Ramallah office. Israel begins building a
separation barrier within the West Bank.

2003: The Quartet Group (the United States, United
Nations, European Union, and Russia) agree on a
"road map for peace." Palestinians pledge full support,
but Israel rejects key points. Violence continues, and
the security barrier in the West Bank draws
international criticism for undermining the peace
process. An unofficial peace agreement negotiated by
Israelis and Palestinians is released with extensive
international support as the Geneva Initiative.

2004: Yasir Arafat dies.

2005: Mahmoud Abbas (Abu Mazen) is elected president
of the Palestinian National Authority. Israel

unilaterally evacuates its settlements from the Gaza Strip and four from the West Bank.

January 2006:  Ariel Sharon suffers a massive stroke. Palestinians elect a new government, with Hamas winning a small plurality of votes but a majority of parliamentary seats. Israel and the United States isolate Palestine, cutting off funds.

March–August 2006:  Ehud Olmert becomes Israel's prime minister, promising that the dividing wall will, in effect, be the new Israeli–West Bank border. Hamas and Hezbollah militants capture Israeli soldiers, and Israeli forces attack Gaza and Lebanon. Hezbollah missiles strike northern Israel. The United Nations approves Resolution 1701, establishing a fragile cease-fire.

————•◆•————

# PROSPECTS FOR PEACE

One of the major goals of my life, while in political office and since I was retired from the White House by the 1980 election, has been to help ensure a lasting peace for Israelis and others in the Middle East. Many people share the same dream, and at times my own efforts to achieve this goal have been intertwined with some of theirs. It will be good to consider what has brought us to the present situation, the obstacles before us, and some things that can and must be done to bring peace and justice to the region.

No fictional drama could be filled with more excitement, unanticipated happenings, or intriguing characters than this effort to end the ongoing conflict; it is certainly one of the most fascinating and truly important political and military subjects of modern times. The Middle East is perhaps the most volatile region in the world, whose instability is a persistent threat to global peace. It is also the incubator of much of the terrorism that is of such great concern to Americans and citizens of other nations. Although it is not difficult to express the challenges in somewhat simplistic terms, the issues are extremely complex and are derived from both ancient and modern-day political and religious history.

The questions to be considered are almost endless:

What are the prime requisites for peace? What possibilities does the future hold? What common ground already exists on which the contending parties can build a more secure future? Are there better prospects for success from quiescent diplomatic efforts or from bold and public pressure for negotiations? Can there be a stable peace that perpetuates the present circumstances? Must the situation steadily deteriorate until another crisis causes the interested parties to act? Even with full American backing, can Israel's enormous military power prevail over militant Arabs?

Most chilling of all, could the festering differences precipitate a military confrontation involving the use of nuclear weapons? It is known that Israel has a major nuclear arsenal and the capability to launch weapons quickly, and some neighboring states are believed to be attempting to acquire their own atomic bombs. Without progress toward peace, desperation or adventurism on either side could precipitate such a confrontation.

There are growing schisms in the Middle East region, with hardening Arab animosity toward the Israeli–United States alliance. The war in Iraq has dramatized the conflict between Sunni and Shia Muslims, and has strengthened the influence of Iran. Militant Arabs, including Hamas and Hezbollah, have been given new life and influence as they are seen to be struggling against Israeli occupation of Palestine. The absence of any viable peace initiative exacerbates each individual controversy.

In times of greatest discouragement, ultimate hope has rested on the fact that, overwhelmingly, the people in the region—even those Syrians, Israelis, Lebanese, and Palestinians who are most distrusted by their adversaries—want the peace efforts to succeed. The rhetoric and demands from all sides may be harsh, but there are obvious areas of agreement that can provide a basis for progress. Private discussions with Arab leaders are much more promising than their public statements would lead one to believe, and in Israel there is a strong and persistent constituency for moderation that is too little heard or appreciated in neighboring states or in America.

Continuing impediments have been the desire of some Israelis for Palestinian land, the refusal of some Arabs to accept Israel as a neighbor, the absence of a clear and authoritative Palestinian voice acceptable to Israel, the refusal of both sides to join peace talks without onerous preconditions, the rise in Islamic fundamentalism, and the recent lack of any protracted effort by the United States to pursue peace based on international law and previous agreements ratified by Israel.

In spite of the obvious need to resolve differences, the peace effort does not have a life of its own; it is not self-sustaining. The United States will always be preoccupied with Iraq, Iran, North Korea, or other strategic responsibilities, and there are competing factors that distract Arab leaders who heretofore had been more inclined to focus on peace with Israel and a just solution to the Palestinian question. Many Arab regimes have become increasingly preoccupied with domestic problems, which include resurgent religious identity, rising expectations among more literate constituencies and the emerging middle classes, a fear of further intrusion by external forces, and stirrings of democracy. There is a tendency for these regimes to free themselves from their Palestinian burden.

The situation is obviously not encouraging, but neither is it hopeless if leaders can remember the progress already made and build on past negotiated agreements. Most Arab regimes have accepted the permanent existence of Israel as an indisputable fact and are no longer calling for an end to the State of Israel, having contrived a common statement at an Arab summit in 2002 that offers peace and normal relations with Israel for its withdrawal from all Arab territories occupied since 1967, its acceptance of an independent Palestinian state with East Jerusalem as its capital, and its agreement to a just solution of the Palestinian refugee problem.

There is no place for sustained violence, which tends to

subvert peace initiatives and perpetuate hatred and combat. Some Palestinians have responded to political and military occupation by launching terrorist attacks against Israeli civilians, a course of action that is both morally reprehensible and politically counterproductive. These dastardly acts have brought widespread condemnation and discredit on the entire Palestinian community—and are almost suicidal for the Palestinian cause. It has been encouraging to observe an almost complete absence of violence during those all-too-brief intervals when the prospects for peace and justice gave the people hope. This was evident, for instance, during the time of the Camp David Accords in 1978, and when the Palestinians were welcomed to the Madrid conference in 1991, as well as during the several Palestinian elections.

It has always been clear that the antagonists cannot be expected to take the initiative to resolve their own differences. Hatred and distrust in the Middle East are too ingrained and pride is too great for any of the disputing parties to offer invitations or concessions that they know will almost inevitably be rejected. Accommodation must be sought through negotiation with all parties to the dispute, with each having fair representation and the right to participate in free discussions. Compromise is necessary from both sides, with clear distinctions made between what their dreams and ideology dictate and what is pragmatically possible. Although some extremists disagree, most Israelis have learned that they cannot reconstruct the Kingdom of David, which includes all of the West Bank, the Golan Heights, and parts of Lebanon and Jordan. At the same time, most Palestinians have been forced to accept the fact that the nation of Israel will never be erased from the map. Neither side can predict or impose on others the ultimate outcome of negotiations, and any final agreement has to be both voluntary and acceptable to both sides.

Strong support for peace talks must come from the United States, preferably involving representatives of the United Nations, the European Union, and Russia. Until recently, America's leaders were known and expected to exert maximum influence in an objective, nonbiased way to achieve peace in the Middle East. In order to resume this vital role, the United States must be a trusted participant, evenhanded, consistent, unwavering, and enthusiastic—a partner with both sides and not a judge of either. Although it is inevitable that at times there will be a tilt one way or the other, in the long run the role of honest broker must once again be played by Washington.

When a promising negotiation evolves, the United States will have to join other wealthy nations in offering the political and economic incentives necessary to bolster what will be at first a fragile understanding and then be prepared to help the peacemakers fend off the radicals and extremists who will seek to subvert what is being carefully created and nurtured.

The three most basic premises are quite clear:

1. Israel's right to exist within recognized borders—and to live in peace—must be accepted by Palestinians and all other neighbors;

2. The killing of noncombatants in Israel, Palestine, and Lebanon by bombs, missile attacks, assassinations, or other acts of violence cannot be condoned; and

3. Palestinians must live in peace and dignity in their own land as specified by international law unless modified by good-faith negotiations with Israel.

The recent outbreak of violence in Gaza and between Israel and Lebanon is vivid proof of the need for a comprehensive peace agreement. The United States stands almost alone in its undeviating backing of Israel, while Arab support for militant groups approaches unanimity as violence continues. People of most other nations strongly condemn the excessive destruction and civilian casualties by Israel as they deplore the deliberate provocation of Israel by Hamas and Hezbollah.

In the final analysis, the different peoples of the Middle East have their own viewpoints, their own grievances, their own goals and aspirations. But it is Israel that remains the key, the tiny vortex around which swirl the winds of hatred, intolerance, and bloodshed. The indomitable people of Israel are still attempting to define their future, the basic character of their nation, its geographical boundaries, and conditions under which the legitimate rights of the Palestinians can be honored and an accommodation forged with its neighbors. These internal decisions will have to be made in consultation with Arabs who are basically antagonistic—perhaps as difficult a political prospect as history has ever seen. Many Israelis, like their neighbors, are eagerly seeking a measure of normalized existence, but the verbal threats from Iran and some radical Arabs and the terrorist attacks in the occupied territories and even within Israel have kept alive the feelings of distrust and alienation among Israelis toward their neighbors. The most extreme and obnoxious statements have come from Iranian President Mahmoud Ahmadinejad, who has described the Holocaust as "a myth" and urged that Israel be annihilated or moved from the Middle East to Europe.

The Arabs must recognize the reality that is Israel, just as the Israelis must accept a Palestinian state in the small remaining portion of territorial homeland allotted to the Palestinians by the United Nations and previous peace agreements. Palestinian human rights must be protected as generally recognized under international law, including self-determination, free speech, equal treatment of all persons, freedom from prolonged military domination and imprisonment without trial, the right of families to be reunited, the sanctity of ownership of property, and the right of non-belligerent people to live in peace.

The Bible says that when the first blood was shed among

His children, God asked Cain, the slayer, "Where is Abel thy brother?" And he said, "I know not. Am I my brother's keeper?" And the Lord said, "What hast thou done? The voice of thy brother's blood crieth unto me from the ground. And now art thou cursed . . ." (Genesis 4:9–11). The blood of Abraham,* God's father of the chosen, still flows in the veins of Arab, Jew, and Christian, and too much of it has been spilled in grasping for the inheritance of the revered patriarch in the Middle East. The spilled blood in the Holy Land still cries out to God—an anguished cry for peace.

It will be seen that there is a formula for peace with justice in this small and unique portion of the world. It is compatible with international law and sustained American government policy, has the approval of most Israelis and Palestinians, and conforms to agreements previously consummated—but later renounced. It is this blueprint that we will now explore.

---

*I used this phrase as the title of my earlier book about the Middle East, *The Blood of Abraham* (Boston: Houghton-Mifflin, 1985; repr. Fayetteville, AR: University of Arkansas Press, 1993).

# 2

———— • ◆ • ————

# MY FIRST VISIT
# TO ISRAEL,
# 1973

I have visited Israel many times and have discussed existing circumstances and future prospects with strong-willed persons who represent many different points of view, both Israelis at home and Jews in other countries who retain an intense interest in the nation and its policies. I have continued to learn both during and after my years in the White House, but even before I was president, I established personal relationships with Yitzhak Rabin, Moshe Dayan, Golda Meir, Abba Eban, and other Israeli leaders and learned all I could about Israel and its political and military challenges. Since this is when I formed most of my lasting impressions of Israel, I'll cover these early experiences in some detail.

My personal introduction to Israel came at a time when

its citizens were filled with confidence and optimism about their future. During its early years, Israel had appeared vulnerable to punishing Arab attacks, but the 1967 war demonstrated that its forces were far more effective than those of its neighbors. The Israeli air force destroyed most of the opposition, and land forces moved south and west through the Gaza Strip and the arid Sinai desert to the Suez Canal, east to the Jordan River to occupy the West Bank, and northeast to take the Golan Heights. One of the heroes of the war was General Yitzhak Rabin. As part of an effort by Israel to strengthen even further its relationship with American leaders, he came to Georgia when I was governor. He seemed pleased to answer my eager questions about military and political relationships in the Middle East and invited me to visit Israel at an early date as his guest.

Having studied Bible lessons since early childhood and taught them for twenty years, I was infatuated with the Holy Land, and my wife, Rosalynn, and I arranged to accept his invitation in 1973. In preparing for this trip, we pored over maps and reviewed both the ancient and modern history of Israel. Our choice of how to spend the ten-day visit was a series of compromises because I was torn between the pleasure of visiting the Christian holy places I had always longed to see and the knowledge that I should concentrate on preparing for another political career. With only a handful of my closest friends knowing of my dreams, I was seriously planning a future role as president.

We first met briefly with Prime Minister Golda Meir, who assigned us a used Mercedes station wagon and a young student as driver. Her instructions were that we would have seven days to travel to any places of our choice, and during the last three days we would receive what she described as confidential briefings on Israel's security interests and relationships with other nations in the region. She wanted our final visit to be with her, so she could answer any questions and summarize the message of her government.

Our driver's name was Giora Avidar; he was a very knowledgeable young son of a diplomat. He gave me an elementary guidebook to the Hebrew language, and I practiced reading the road signs as we traveled from place to place. I still have the booklet, in which I made notes during our visit. I have also retained a map of Israel that he provided. There is no indication of a "green line" between Israel and the West Bank or Gaza, and the map also includes a substantial portion of the Golan Heights and all of the Sinai. There was an expressed desire among some radical Israelis to retain the captured territories, but the prevailing attitude among the nation's leaders was that the occupied lands should be kept only until they could be traded for a secure peace with the Arabs. None of my official briefings included plans for permanent retention or early withdrawal.

We spent our first three days in and around Jerusalem, beginning each morning before sunrise, because I wanted to see the city come to life when few tourists were about and to catch a flavor of how it might have been two thousand years earlier, when Jesus strolled the same streets. We visited the bakeries where bread was prepared for the market in large open ovens, sipped coffee or tea in the small shops, and watched vendors arrange their wares for the unfolding day. I had long talks with archaeologists who were excavating in the biblical City of David, and they described how the detritus of past civilizations had constantly raised the level of the streets on an average of about one foot a century. This made it easier for us to understand why the holy sites we visited in Jerusalem, Bethlehem, Hebron, Jericho, and Nazareth were so different from what we had expected. They seemed buried belowground, closed in, tinseled, and highly commercial, not simple and primitive, as we had always imagined. Only when we traveled in the open spaces and saw the Mount of Olives, the Garden Tomb, Cana, Mount Carmel, the Sea of Galilee, the Mount of Beatitudes, Capernaum, Bethsaida, and the Jordan River did we feel that we were looking at the country as it might have appeared in biblical times.

As we arrived at each destination, Giora introduced us as special guests of Prime Minister Meir and General Rabin, and our hosts seemed eager to answer our questions and make us feel welcome and at home. Our most enjoyable and informative outing was in Nazareth. After visiting the Church of the Annunciation and the subterranean dwellings that were said to typify those where Jesus lived, we were guests at an exciting and somewhat boisterous lunch with the Muslim mayor, his Christian deputy, the Jewish mayor of Upper Nazareth, and a number of their families and friends. For several hours we ate prodigious quantities of lamb that had been roasted whole, fruit, vegetables, bread, and a thick stew that we scooped up with our fingers. I remember that there were several bottles of Johnnie Walker Red Label scotch down the center of the long table, largely consumed during the numerous toasts offered on every conceivable subject, and later we drank the thick black coffee typical of the region.

We were intrigued with how the officials of Nazareth were striving to increase tourism and promote economic progress, and in the afternoon we went over to the new city being built to house some of the recent immigrants from the Soviet Union, who seemed to be arriving in a steady stream. The wall paint was hardly dry when each family moved into their new apartment, and there were plans to build three thousand more units to house those yet to come. Immigration had increased following Israel's victory in the 1967 war, reaching its highest level the year we were there. The mayor said that up to a hundred factories around metropolitan Nazareth would provide jobs for both the old and new residents. Some of the longtime citizens complained about the special treatment being given to the newcomers, but these dissident voices were not widespread or persistent. We talked to several of the Soviet settlers, who bragged to the younger ones that they had begun studying Hebrew from the first day in their new homes.

We continued our travels to Cana and then along the paths of Jesus in his early ministry to Capernaum and other communities around the Sea of Galilee. It was especially interesting to visit with some of the few surviving Samaritans, who complained to us that their holy sites and culture were not being respected by Israeli authorities—the same complaint heard by Jesus and his disciples almost two thousand years earlier.

Later we visited several kibbutzim (collective farms or settlements), one of them already fifty-four years old. As a farmer, I was interested to learn that they grew apples and were able to keep them in cold storage for sale almost year-round and that their cows were milked three times daily (instead of the usual two milkings) to increase production and profits. The next morning was the Sabbath, and at the appointed time we entered the synagogue, said a silent prayer, and then stood quietly just inside the door. Only two other worshipers appeared. When I asked if this was typical, Giora gave a wry smile and shrugged his shoulders as if it was not important either way.

We obtained a different perspective when we visited a settlement on the Golan Heights, taken from Syria in 1967. There we found much more of a pioneer spirit and were impressed by the quiet dedication of the young families who farmed together. They seemed to share everything and were quite proud of their hard manual labor and the absence of worldly goods in their homes. The kibbutz leaders took us to the steep western slope overlooking Galilee to show us gun emplacements that had been built and used by the Syrians against the Israelis during the 1967 war. We could see far below us the small villages along the lakeshore, homes in the valley, automobiles on the roads, and tractors cultivating the fields. It was obvious why control of this site was so important to Israel militarily, pending a peace agreement with Syria. The young Israelis spoke with growing fervor, explaining that the strength of Israel was being tested every day and must never be found wanting. They were convinced that their own kibbutz was valuable both economically and militarily and made it clear to us that they intended never to have enemy guns firing down on Israelis from these cliffs again.

There were only about 1,500 Jewish settlers in the occupied territories at that time, and our natural presumption was that Israel would dismantle the unwanted settlements to comply with international law, including U.N. Security Council resolutions that had been supported by both Israel and the United States. I knew that Prime Minister Meir had said that there were no separate Palestinian people, but we assumed this to mean there should be no future racial delineation between Jews and Gentiles.

I have to admit that, at the time, I equated the ejection of Palestinians from their previous homes within the State of

Israel to the forcing of Lower Creek Indians from the Georgia land where our family farm was now located; they had been moved west to Oklahoma on the "Trail of Tears" to make room for our white ancestors. In this most recent case, although equally harsh, the taking of land had been ordained by the international community through an official decision of the United Nations. The Palestinians had to comply and, after all, they could return or be compensated in the future, and they were guaranteed undisputed ownership of East Jerusalem, the West Bank, and Gaza.

After going to sea on one of the missile boats that had been spirited from the French despite the post-1967 arms embargo against Israel, we drove east and then south as close as we could to the Jordan River. All our lives we had studied and sung about this stream, so we visualized a mighty current with almost magical qualities. We were amazed to find that it was not as large as the small creeks that flow through our own farm. We learned that much of the water was being diverted from the stream to irrigate Israeli crops—then one of the prime causes of the animosity between Israel and its eastern neighbors. Barbed wire and roadblocks kept us away from the security zone along the river's banks, but with special permission from a border security guard, I took a quick dip in the Jordan River near where I thought Jesus had been baptized by John the Baptist.

At the Allenby Bridge, which crossed the stream, we watched for a while as large numbers of people and vehicles moved to and from Jordan. The customs officials told us that only routine security checks were being made, and during the last three years, they said, more than three-quarters of a million Arabs had visited Israel legally. With a wink, one of the guards added that they could only estimate how many illegal visitors there had been, but that some of them (referring to captured terrorists) had never been able to return home to Jordan.

Later, all of us experienced the extraordinary buoyancy as we swam in the Dead Sea. We noticed that the bathhouses were somewhat distant from the shore, and the attendant said that the water level had been dropping as more and more irrigation systems tapped the dwindling stream. He said there would ultimately be two small seas if the trend continued.

After we finished our ambitious itinerary as tourists, we followed the schedule that had been prepared by Israeli officials. We went with General Rabin to Bethel, a training camp in the occupied territories where I was asked to participate in a military graduation ceremony. This facility in the West Bank had been used by the Jordanians for the same purpose before Israel occupied the area in the Six-Day War. The soldiers stood rigidly at attention, and, as each name was called, the graduate ran at top speed to the reviewing stand, where the commander delivered a diploma and I presented a "Sword of the Spirit" (a Hebrew Bible), which was one of the few indications of a religious commitment that I observed during our visit.

General Rabin described the close relationship that Israel had with South Africa in the diamond trade (he had returned from there a day or two early to greet us) but commented that the South African system of apartheid could not long survive. When I asked about his own political future, he said that he would have a place on the Labor Party list but had not yet been assured of a cabinet post.

At that time, Foreign Minister Abba Eban was the best-known Israeli, famous for the eloquence of his speeches in the United Nations, and I was excited when he invited us to meet with him. Not surprisingly, he was full of ideas about Israel's future, some of which proved to be remarkably prescient. He said that the occupied territories were a burden and not an asset. Arabs and Jews were inherently incompatible and would ultimately have to be separated. The detention centers and associated punitive and repressive procedures necessary to govern hundreds of thousands of Arabs against their will would torment Israel with a kind of quasi-colonial situation that was being abolished throughout the rest of the world. When questioned, he replied without explanation that the solution to this problem was being evolved. (I knew that some Israeli leaders were contemplating massive immigration from both Russia and the United States plus encouraging Arabs to emigrate to other nations.) Eban explained his extraordinary role in the United Nations by saying, "If I were foreign minister of the only Arab nation surrounded by thirty-nine hostile Jewish ones, I would turn to the U.N. for support."

Major General Eliahu Zeira, head of Israeli military intelligence, and Army Chief of Staff Haim Bar Lev gave me private and "top secret" briefings on the military and political situation in the neighboring countries, with an emphasis on Syria and Egypt. Again and again they referred to the 1967 war as an example of Israel's invulnerability and left no doubt that they were thoroughly prepared for any eventuality. Although only 5 percent of Israeli military personnel were kept in uniform, their intelligence was excellent and the mobilization time for reserve troops would be very brief. Describing their "defensive" military forces, the top commanders acknowledged the vital alliance with the United States but emphasized Israel's self-sufficiency if given adequate supplies and permission to produce their own versions of U.S. aircraft, tanks, and other military materiel. I presumed that this message was one of the reasons for my invitation to visit.

During our final hours in Jerusalem we were invited to attend a session of the Knesset, where Prime Minister Meir addressed the assembly. I commented on the No Smoking signs around the auditorium, which everyone was obeying except the prime minister, and Giora explained: "We have a choice to make. Either have no signs and everyone smoking or put up signs and have one person smoke. We decided that one person smoking wouldn't be too bad."

Later, in her office, I thanked the prime minister for making possible our wonderful visit, and she asked if I had any observations I would like to share. With some hesitation, I said that I had long taught lessons from the Hebrew Scriptures and that a common historical pattern was that Israel was punished whenever the leaders turned away from devout worship of God. I asked if she was concerned about the secular nature of her Labor government. She seemed surprised at my temerity and dismissed my comments with a shrug and a laugh. She lit one cigarette from another and then said that "orthodox" Jews still existed and could assume that portion of the nation's responsibility. She was referring to the religious Jews in the Israeli parliament, who were sometimes a real thorn in her side. She added, "If you attend a session of the Knesset, you will see them in action and will know that they have not lost their faith." With Israel's system of elections, which necessitates a coalition of parties to form a ruling majority, the minority religious organizations had an influence far exceeding their numerical strength.

Neither Mrs. Meir nor I realized it then, but Menachem Begin, the leader of the Herut Party with only 22 percent of the Knesset seats, would be prime minister of Israel within four years (and I would be president of the United States). Much of Begin's political strength would come from his deep religious convictions.

Throughout our travels we found the country to be surprisingly relaxed and saw only a handful of people in uniform, mostly directing traffic at the busier intersections. Also, there seemed to be an easy relationship among the different kinds of people we met, including Jews and Arabs. Later, I realized that I had had few personal contacts or political discussions with Arabs who were not living inside Israel, but at the time their plight seemed of relative insignificance to me.

I recorded some of the private and public comments that indicate how the atmosphere in Israel was buoyant with a sense of success and prosperity:

"The United States is our only important friend."

"The Russians now want peace in the Middle East. They cannot afford another major defeat of their Arab allies."

"The Europeans are obsessed with economics. France is our worst enemy in the Common Market—moralistic to a fault."

"Arabs are incompatible with us; they have no loyalty to the Israeli flag. Israeli Arabs are the fastest-growing community on earth, and it's only Jewish immigration that will let us retain a majority."

"The Arab oil weapon is not a real threat. They need dollars more than the world needs their oil. Israel receives 90 percent of its oil needs from the Sinai and Iran. We have no foreseeable problems in obtaining enough fuel."

"No one should fear the Arab nations. They have been badly beaten in every conflict and eventually will have to sue for peace."

We left convinced that the Israelis were dominant but just, the Arabs quiescent because their rights were being protected, and the political and military situation destined to remain stable until land was swapped for peace. I was excited and optimistic about the apparent commitment of the Israelis to establish a nation that would be a homeland for the Jews, dedicated to the Judeo-Christian principles of peace and justice, and determined to live in harmony with all their neighbors. Although aware of the subservient status of the Palestinians, I was reassured by the assumption that Israel would withdraw from the occupied territories in exchange for peace. I was reminded of the words of Israel's first president, Chaim Weizmann: "I am certain the world will judge the Jewish state by how it will treat the Arabs."

After returning home, I monitored developments in the Middle East very closely. Absorbed with maintaining their control of the West Bank and continuing to build their economy and world alliances, the Israelis were caught completely by surprise four months after my visit, in October 1973, when Presidents Anwar al-Sadat of Egypt and Hafez al-Assad of Syria orchestrated simultaneous attacks by their forces into the Sinai and the Golan Heights, both occupied by Israel. Well armed with Soviet weapons, the Arabs were at first successful, but Israeli tenacity and additional military supplies from the United States eventually turned the tide.

I was deeply concerned when the combined forces of the superpowers almost came into conflict as Israel's military forces crossed the Suez Canal and were moving toward Cairo, Egypt. The nuclear armadas of the Soviet Union (defending Egypt) and the United States (supporting Israel) were put on high alert for the only time in history. Fortunately, the two great nations used their influence to bring about a cease-fire after twenty days of combat, and Secretary of State Henry Kissinger managed to negotiate permanent disengagement agreements.

# 3

## MY PRESIDENCY, 1977–81

The 1973 war introduced major changes in the character of the Middle East. The effective performance of the Egyptian and Syrian armies increased the stature of both President Anwar al-Sadat of Egypt and President Hafez al-Assad of Syria. The Arab states demonstrated that they were willing to use oil as a weapon in support of Arab interests, through embargo and price increases. In Israel, Prime Minister Golda Meir resigned and, in June 1974, Yitzhak Rabin took her place. Also, in October, Arab leaders unanimously proclaimed the Palestine Liberation Organization as the sole legitimate representative of the Palestinian people, with Yasir Arafat as its leader. Now the Palestinians were to be seen as a people who could speak for themselves.

The PLO became a powerful political entity, able to

arouse strong support in international forums from the Arabs, the Soviet Union, most Third World countries, and many others. However, U.S. government leaders pledged not to recognize or negotiate with the PLO until the organization officially accepted U.N. Resolution 242, which required the acknowledgment of the sovereignty and political independence of every state in the Middle East (including Israel) and their right to live in peace within secure and recognized borders. A more important problem was that the PLO's rejection of Israel was shared by the leaders of all Arab nations, following four wars in the previous twenty-five years.

These were the events that I monitored after returning home from my first visit to Israel and during my race for president. It was a rare day on the campaign trail that I did not receive questions from Jewish citizens about the interests of Israel, and my growing team of issue analysts provided me with briefing papers that I could study. I made repeated promises that I would seek to invigorate the dormant peace effort, and after I was elected and before my inauguration I made a speech at the Smithsonian Institution in which I listed this as a major foreign policy goal.

Since the United States had to play a strong role in any peace effort, I reviewed the official positions of my predecessors on the key issues. Our nation's constant policy had been predicated on a few key United Nations Security Council resolutions, notably 242 of 1967 (Appendix 1) and 338 of 1973 (Appendix 2). Approved unanimously and still applicable, their basic premise is that Israel's acquisition of territory by force is illegal and that Israel must withdraw from occupied territories; that Israel has the right to live in peace within secure and recognized boundaries; that the refugee problem must be settled; and that the international community should assist with negotiations to achieve a just and durable peace in the Middle East. More specifically, U.S. policy was that Israeli settlements in the West Bank and Gaza were "illegal and obstacles to peace." One of my first and most controversial public statements came in March 1977, just a few weeks after I became president, when I reviewed these same premises and added, "There has to be a homeland provided for the Palestinian refugees who have suffered for many, many years." This would be the first move toward supporting a Palestinian state.

Two weeks later, President Sadat came to Washington for a state visit, and after the official banquet he and I went upstairs to the living quarters in the White House. During a long, private conversation it became obvious that his inclination to work with me on peace negotiations was already well developed, but he had not decided on any firm plan to reach what might become our common goal. Sadat told me plainly that he was willing to take bold steps toward peace, all of them based on the prevailing U.N. Security Council resolutions. We discussed some of the specific elements of possible direct negotiations in the future: Israel's permanent boundaries, the status of Jerusalem, Palestinian rights, and—almost inconceivable at the time—free trade and open borders between the two nations, plus full diplomatic recognition and the exchange of ambassadors.

Menachem Begin replaced Yitzhak Rabin as prime minister a month later, and I quickly learned all I could about Israel's new leader. His surprising victory ended the uninterrupted domination of the Labor Party since Israel's independence. Begin had put together a majority coalition that accepted his premise that the land in Gaza and the West Bank belonged rightfully to the State of Israel and should not be exchanged for a permanent peace agreement with the Arabs. Public opinion varied widely, but there was no doubt in 1977 that a more hawkish attitude now prevailed in the government of Israel. I was deeply concerned but sent him personal congratulations and an invitation to visit me in Washington.

Although many factors had influenced the outcome of the Israeli election, age and ethnic differences strongly favored the Likud over the Labor alignment. Oriental Jews (known as Sephardim), whose families had come from the Middle East and Africa, gave the Likud coalition parties a political margin in 1977, and they were inclined to support a much more militant policy in dealing with the occupied territories. Although Begin was not one of them by birth, his philosophy and demeanor were attractive to the Sephardic voters. Also, the Sephardim were generally younger, more conservative, and nearer the bottom of the economic ladder and they resented the more prosperous and sophisticated Jewish immigrants from Europe and America (known as Ashkenazim), who had furnished almost all of Israel's previous leaders. The Sephardic families had a higher birth rate than the Ashkenazim, and now, combined with many immigrants, they had become a strong political force.

The personal character of Menachem Begin was also a major factor in the victory. After he and his family suffered persecution in Eastern Europe and Siberia for his political activity as a Zionist, he was released from a Soviet prison and went to Palestine in 1942. He became the leader of a militant underground group called the Irgun, which espoused the maximum demands of Zionism. These included driving British forces out of Palestine. He fought with every weapon available against the British, who branded him as the preeminent terrorist in the region. A man of personal courage and single-minded devotion to his goals, he took pride in being a "fighting Jew." I realized that Israel's new prime minister, with whom I would be dealing, would be prepared to resort to extreme measures to achieve the goals in which he believed.

In Israel, Begin put forward clear and blunt answers to complex questions about peace and war, religion, the Palestinians, finance, and economics. I expected him to have a clear idea of when he might yield and what he would not give up in negotiations with his Arab neighbors and the United States. However, when he came to Washington to meet with me, I found the prime minister quite willing to pursue some of the major goals that I had discussed with Sadat.

I also had definitive discussions with King Hussein of Jordan and President Assad of Syria, but it was obvious that they would not be willing to participate in the kind of peace effort that Sadat, Begin, and I had discussed. The economic and political pressures among the Arab leaders to maintain a unanimous condemnation of Israel were overwhelming. The PLO was out of diplomatic bounds for me, still officially classified by the United States as a terrorist organization. Despite this restraint, I sought through unofficial channels to induce Arafat to accept the key U.N. resolutions so that the PLO could join in peace efforts, but he refused.

I sent Sadat a handwritten letter telling him how "extremely important—perhaps vital" it was for us to work together, and he and I discussed various possibilities by telephone. In November 1977, Sadat made a dramatic peace initiative by going directly to Jerusalem. Begin received Sadat graciously and listened with apparent composure while the Egyptian president laid down in no uncertain terms the strongest Arab position, which included Israel's immediate withdrawal from all occupied territories and the right of return of Palestinians to their former homes. I found it interesting that Sadat decided not to follow the counsel of his advisers that he make the speech in

English for the world audience, but to deliver it in Arabic for the benefit of his Arab neighbors. The symbolism of his presence obscured the harshness of his actual words, so the reaction in Western nations was overwhelmingly favorable and the Israeli public responded with excitement and enthusiasm. The responses of the Saudis, Jordanians, and some of the other moderate Arab leaders were cautious, but Syria broke diplomatic relations with Egypt, and high officials in Damascus, Baghdad, Tripoli, and the PLO called for Sadat's assassination.

Prime Minister Begin came to the White House to discuss specific peace proposals, and there was a flurry of meetings between the Egyptians and Israelis that culminated shortly after Christmas in a return visit by Begin to Egypt. Sadat reported to me that the session was completely unsatisfactory, an apparently fatal setback for his peace initiative, because Begin was insisting that Israeli settlements must remain on Egyptian land in the Sinai. It appeared that the only permanent result of Sadat's move was an end to any prospect for an international peace conference involving the Soviets. I consulted with as many Arab leaders as possible on a fast New Year's trip to the region and found them somewhat supportive of Sadat in private but quite critical in their public statements, honoring a pledge of unanimity with their other Arab brothers.

During the early part of 1978, Sadat sent me a private message that he intended to come to the United States and publicly condemn Begin as a betrayer of the peace process. Rosalynn and I invited Anwar and his wife, Jehan, to Camp David for a personal visit, and after a weekend of intense talks, Sadat was convinced to cancel his planned speech and join me in search of an agreement.

Unfortunately, my working relationship with Menachem Begin became even more difficult in March, when the PLO launched an attack on Israel from a base in Southern Lebanon. A sightseeing bus was seized and thirty-five Israelis were killed. I publicly condemned this outrageous act, but my sympathy was strained three days later when Israel invaded Lebanon and used American-made antipersonnel cluster bombs against Beirut and other urban centers, killing hundreds of civilians and leaving thousands homeless. I considered this major invasion to be an overreaction to the PLO attack, a serious threat to peace in the region, and perhaps part of a plan to establish a permanent Israeli presence in Southern Lebanon. Also, such use of American weapons violated a legal requirement that armaments sold by us be used only for Israeli defense against an attack.

After consulting with key supporters of Israel in the U.S. Senate, I informed Prime Minister Begin that if Israeli forces remained in Lebanon, I would have to notify Congress, as required by law, that U.S. weapons were being used illegally in Lebanon, which would automatically cut off all military aid to Israel. Also, I instructed the State Department to prepare a U.N. Security Council resolution condemning Israel's action. Israeli forces withdrew, and United Nations troops came in to replace them in Southern Lebanon, adequate to restrain further PLO attacks on Israeli citizens.

Our efforts to rejuvenate the overall peace process were fruitless during the spring and summer. My next act was almost one of desperation. I decided to invite both Begin and Sadat to Camp David so that we could be away from routine duties for a few days and, in relative isolation, I could act as mediator between the two national delegations. They accepted without delay, and on September 4 we began what evolved into a thirteen-day session, which involved teams of about fifty on each side. My aim was to have Israelis and Egyptians understand and accept the compatibility of many of their goals and the advantages to both nations in resolving their differences. We had to address such basic questions as Israeli withdrawal from the occupied territories, Palestinian rights, Israel's security, an end to the Arab trade embargo, open borders between Israel and Egypt, the rights of Israeli ships to transit the Suez Canal, and the sensitive issues concerning sovereignty over Jerusalem and access to the holy places. In the process, I hoped to achieve a permanent peace between the two countries based on full diplomatic recognition as would be confirmed by a bilateral peace treaty.

Begin and Sadat were personally incompatible, and I decided after a few unpleasant encounters that they should not attempt to negotiate with each other. Instead, I worked during the last ten days and nights with each or with their representatives separately. Although this approach was more difficult for me—I had to go from one negotiating session to another—there were advantages in that it avoided the harsh rhetoric and personal arguing between the two leaders. At least with Begin, every word of the final agreement was carefully considered, and he and I spent a lot of time perusing a thesaurus and a dictionary. He was a careful semanticist. He surprised me once when I had proposed autonomy for the Palestinians; he insisted on "*full* autonomy."*

Begin came to Camp David intending just to work out a statement of broad, general principles for a peace agreement, leaving to subordinates the task of resolving the more difficult details. It was soon obvious that he was more interested in discussing the Sinai than the West Bank and Gaza, and he spent the best part of his energy on the minute details of each proposal. The other key members of the Israeli team, Foreign Minister Moshe Dayan, Defense Minister Ezer Weizman, and Attorney General Aharon Barak, desired as full an agreement as possible with the Egyptians, and they were often able to convince Begin that a particular proposal was beneficial to Israel and would be approved by its citizens.

*For a more complete day-by-day description of the Camp David negotiations, see Jimmy Carter, *Keeping Faith: Memoirs of a President* (New York: Bantam, 1982), pp. 319–403; (repr. Fayetteville, AR: University of Arkansas Press, 1995), pp. 326–412.

Sadat wanted a comprehensive peace agreement, and he was the most forthcoming member of the Egyptian delegation. His general requirements were that all Israelis leave the Egyptian Sinai and that there be a comprehensive accord involving the occupied territories, Palestinian rights, and Israel's commitment to resolve peacefully any further disputes with its neighbors. Both sides would have to pledge to honor U.N. Resolution 242. Sadat usually left the details of the negotiations to me or the key negotiator of his Egyptian team, Osama el-Baz.

On several occasions either Begin or Sadat was ready to terminate the discussions and return home, but we finally negotiated the Camp David Accords (Appendix 3), including the framework of a peace treaty between the two nations (Appendix 4). The two leaders and their advisers even agreed upon my carefully worded paragraph on the most sensitive issue of all, the Holy City:

> Jerusalem, the city of peace, is holy to Judaism, Christianity, and Islam, and all peoples must have free access to it and enjoy the free exercise of worship and the right to visit and transit to the holy places without distinction or discrimination. The holy places of each faith will be under the administration and control of their representatives. A municipal council representative of the inhabitants of the city shall supervise essential functions in the city such as

public utilities, public transportation, and tourism and shall ensure that each community can maintain its own cultural and educational institutions.

At the last minute, however, after several days of unanimous agreement, both Sadat and Begin decided that there were already enough controversial elements in the Accords and requested that this paragraph be deleted from the final text.

It is to be remembered that the Camp David Accords, signed by Sadat and Begin and officially ratified by both governments, reconfirmed a specific commitment to honor U.N. Resolutions 242 and 338, which prohibit acquisition of land by force and call for Israel's withdrawal from occupied territories. The Accords prescribe "full autonomy" for inhabitants of the occupied territories, withdrawal of Israeli military and civilian forces from the West Bank and Gaza, and the recognition of the Palestinian people as a separate political entity with a right to determine their own future, a major step toward a Palestinian state. They specify that Palestinians are to participate as equals in further negotiations, and the final status of the West Bank and Gaza is to be submitted "to a vote by the elected representatives of the inhabitants of the West Bank and Gaza." Furthermore, the Accords generally recognized that continuing to treat non-Jews in the occupied territories as a substratum of society is contrary to the principles

# Map 4

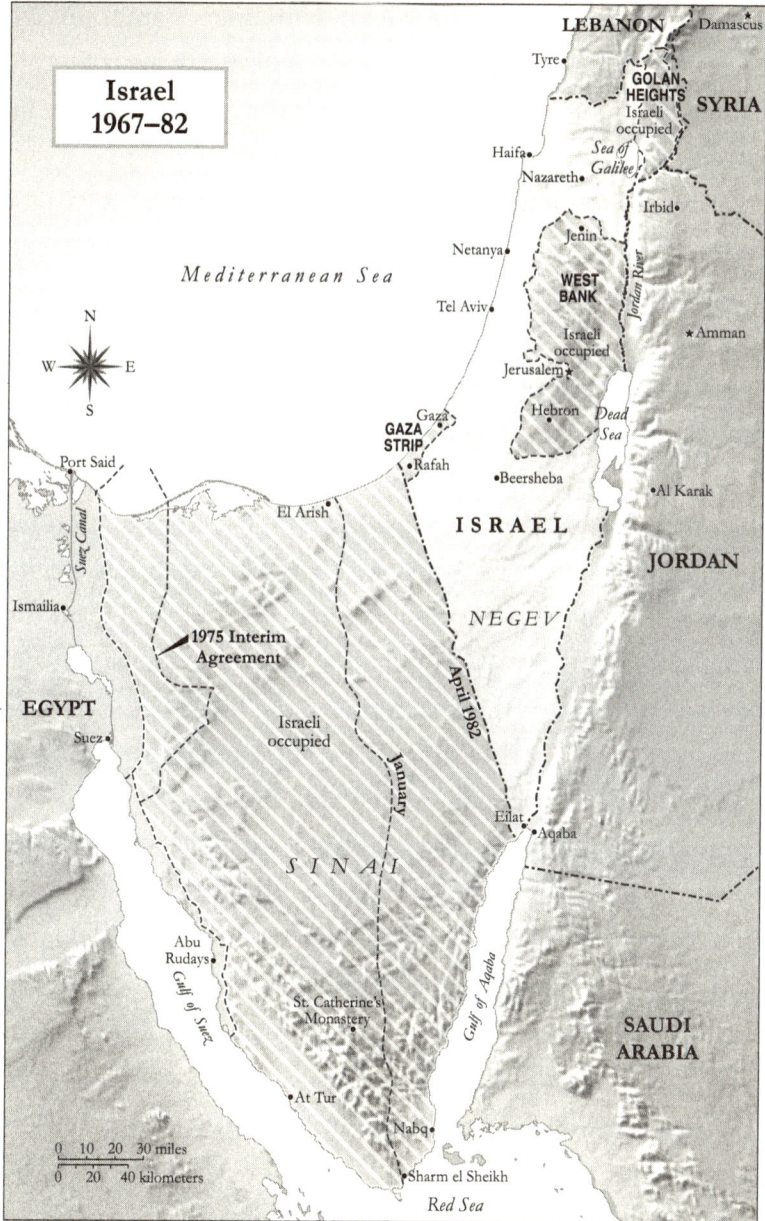

Israel
1967–82

LEBANON · Damascus

Tyre

GOLAN
HEIGHTS
Israeli
occupied

SYRIA

Haifa

Sea of
Galilee

Nazareth

Irbid

Netanya

Jenin

Mediterranean Sea

WEST
BANK

Jordan River

N
W E
S

Tel Aviv

Israeli
occupied

Amman

Jerusalem

Gaza

Hebron

Dead
Sea

Port Said

GAZA
STRIP

Rafah

El Arish

Beersheba

Al Karak

Suez Canal

ISRAEL

Ismailia

JORDAN

NEGEV

1975 Interim
Agreement

April 1982

EGYPT

Suez

Israeli
occupied

Eilat

Aqaba

January

S I N A I

Abu
Rudays

Gulf of Suez

St. Catherine's
Monastery

Gulf of Aqaba

SAUDI
ARABIA

At Tur

Nabq

0  10  20  30 miles
0   20   40 kilometers

Sharm el Sheikh

Red Sea

*49*

JIMMY CARTER

of morality and justice on which democracies are founded. Begin and Sadat agreed that these apparently insurmountable problems concerning Palestinian rights would be overcome.

In addition, the framework for an Egyptian-Israeli peace agreement was signed, calling for withdrawal of Israeli armed forces from the Sinai, diplomatic relations between Israel and Egypt, borders open to trade and commerce, Israeli ships guaranteed passage through the Suez Canal, and a permanent peace treaty to confirm these agreements.

Sadat always insisted that the first priority must be adherence to U.N. Resolution 242 and self-determination for the Palestinians, and everyone (perhaps excepting Begin) was convinced that these rights had been protected in the final document. All of us (including the prime minister) were also confident that the final terms of the treaty could be concluded within the three-month target time. Everyone knew that if Israel began building new settlements, the promise to grant the Palestinians "full autonomy," with an equal or final voice in determining the ultimate status of the occupied territories, would be violated. Perhaps the most serious omission of the Camp David talks was the failure to clarify in writing Begin's verbal promise concerning the settlement freeze during subsequent peace talks.

One personal benefit to me from the long days of negotiation was a lifetime friendship with Ezer Weizman, who served as Israel's defense minister. More than any other member of Begin's team, I found Ezer eager to reach a comprehensive peace agreement, and he was a person with whom I could discuss very sensitive issues with frankness and confidence. He also had a good personal relationship with the Egyptians and would often go by Sadat's cabin for private discussions or a game of backgammon. These peace talks proved to be something of an epiphany for Weizman, who had been an early member of Begin's Irgun team of Zionist militants, a noted hero of the Six-Day War as director of the early morning strikes that decimated the Arab air forces, and a founder of the conservative Likud political party. He had been a leading "hawk" all his life but was converted during the weeks of negotiations into a strong proponent of reconciliation with the Arabs.*

Our celebration of the Camp David Accords was short-lived, as we endured weeks of tedious and frustrating negotiations to implement our commitment to conclude a peace treaty between Israel and Egypt. Six months after Camp David, I decided to go to Cairo and Jerusalem to try to resolve the remaining issues, and we were able to conclude the final terms of a definitive agreement. Although this crucial peace treaty has never been violated, other equally important provisions of our agreement have not been honored

---

*Without my asking him, Ezer Weizman came to America during my re-election campaign in 1980 and visited several cities, publicly urging Jewish leaders to support my candidacy. Although strongly criticized for this unprecedented (and perhaps illegal) foreign involvement, he was undeterred.

since I left office. The Israelis have never granted any appreciable autonomy to the Palestinians, and instead of withdrawing their military and political forces, Israeli leaders have tightened their hold on the occupied territories.

Sadat withstood the condemnation of his fellow Arabs, who imposed severe though ultimately unsuccessful diplomatic, economic, and trade sanctions against Egypt in an attempt to isolate and punish him. Until much later, long after I left public office, neither the Jordanians nor the PLO were willing to participate in subsequent peace talks with Israel. This confirmed the Israelis' fears that their nation's existence would again be threatened as soon as their adversaries could accumulate enough strength to mount a military challenge.

For Menachem Begin, the peace treaty with Egypt was the significant act for Israel, while solemn promises regarding the West Bank and Palestinians would be finessed or deliberately violated. With the bilateral treaty, Israel removed Egypt's considerable strength from the military equation of the Middle East and thus it permitted itself renewed freedom to pursue the goals of a fervent and dedicated minority of its citizens to confiscate, settle, and fortify the occupied territories. Israeli settlement activity still caused great concern, and in 1980, U.N. Resolution 465 (Appendix 5), calling on Israel to dismantle existing settlements in the Arab territories occupied since 1967, including East Jerusalem, was passed unanimously.

We all knew that Israel must have a comprehensive and lasting peace, and this dream could have been realized if Israel had complied with the Camp David Accords and refrained from colonizing the West Bank, with Arabs accepting Israel within its legal borders.

# 4

THE KEY PLAYERS

## THE PALESTINIANS

To understand present circumstances in the Middle East, it is necessary to take a closer look at the Palestinians and the Israelis. We can begin with a brief general description of the Palestinians, whose future status must be a focal point for progress toward peace.

What is Palestine, and who are the Palestinians? The borders of this contentious area, also called the Land of Canaan or the Holy Land, have never been conclusively defined. The name is an ancient one, derived from the Philistines, who lived along the Mediterranean seacoast and were also known as People of the Sea. The Bible does not portray these people very attractively, because they did not worship God and they competed with the authors and heroes of the scriptures for control over parts of Canaan.

Formidable warriors and some of the earliest users of iron weaponry, they were usually able to prevail over their enemies—even the powerful King David. Roman conquerors, after smashing the Second Jewish Revolt in A.D. 135, set out to obliterate the historic Jewish presence in the land. They changed the name of Jerusalem to Aelia Capitolina, and Judaea became the province of Syria Palaestina, later simply Palaestina. When Christianity became the religion of the Roman Empire, the name of Jerusalem was revived. The name Palaestina, translated into Arabic as Filistin, survived the seventh-century Arab conquest, and the name prevailed even as the borders of the region have fluctuated through the centuries.

A succession of Turks, Kurds, and European Crusaders ruled Palestine until the Ottoman Turks incorporated Palestine into their empire in 1516. They were on the losing side in World War I, and France and Great Britain initially assumed authority over the various parts of the Middle East. The League of Nations assigned to Great Britain the supervision of the Mandate of Palestine, which we now know as the lands of Israel, the West Bank, Gaza, and Jordan. After Jordan was separated from the Mandate in 1922, the remaining territory between the Jordan River and the Mediterranean Sea became known as Palestine.

Although Christian and Muslim Arabs had continued to live in this same land since Roman times, they had no real commitment to establish a separate and independent nation.

Their concern was with family and tribe and, for the Muslims, the broader world of Islam. Strong ideas of nationhood began to take shape among the Arabs only when they saw increasing numbers of Zionists immigrate to Palestine, buying tracts of land for permanent homes with the goal of establishing their own nation.

In 1947 the United Nations approved a partition plan for Palestine. A Jewish state was to include 55 percent of this territory (Map 2), Jerusalem and Bethlehem were to be internationalized as holy sites, and the remainder of the land was to constitute an Arab state. The Jewish Agency (an official group that represented the Jewish community in Palestine to the British Mandate) and other Zionist representatives approved the plan, but Arab leaders were almost unanimous in their opposition. When Jews declared their independence as a nation, the Arabs attacked militarily but were defeated. The 1949 armistice demarcation lines became the borders of the new nation of Israel and were accepted by Israel and the United States, and recognized officially by the United Nations.

Israelis had taken 77 percent of the disputed land, and the Palestinians were left with two small separate areas, to be known as the West Bank (annexed by Jordan) and Gaza (administered by Egypt). Jews who lived within their new nation took the name Israelis, while Christian and Muslim Arabs in the Holy Land outside of Israel preferred to be known as Palestinians. The Palestinians' own most expansive definition includes "all those, and their descendants, who were residents of the land before 14 May 1948 [when Israel became a state]."

When Britain conducted a census in Palestine in 1922, there were about 84,000 Jews and 670,000 Arabs, of whom 71,000 were Christians. By the time the area was partitioned by the United Nations, these numbers had grown to about 600,000 Jews and 1.3 million Arabs, 10 percent of whom were Christians. During and after the 1948 war, about 420 Palestinian villages in the territory that became the State of Israel were destroyed and some 700,000 Palestinian residents fled or were driven out.

The Palestinians and individual Arab leaders continued their vehement objections to the increasing Israeli encroachment on what they considered to be their lands and rights. However, it was not until the announcement of Israel's plans to divert water from the Sea of Galilee and the Jordan River to irrigate western Israel and the Negev desert that the first summit meeting of Arab leaders took place early in 1964 and the Palestine Liberation Organization (PLO) was formally organized. The United Nations estimated that by this time there were 1.3 million Palestinian refugees, with one-fourth in Jordan, about 150,000 each in Lebanon and Syria, and most of the others in West Bank and Gaza refugee camps.

In May 1967, after military clashes between Syria and Israel, Egypt blockaded the Straits of Tiran and ordered the removal of U.N. Emergency Forces stationed along the Israel-Egypt border. Other Arab states put their troops on alert. On June 5, Israel launched preemptive strikes, moving first against Egypt and Syria, then against Jordan. Within six days Israeli military forces had occupied the Golan Heights, Gaza, the Sinai, Jerusalem, and the West Bank.

As a result of that conflict, 320,000 more Arabs were forced to leave the additional areas in Syria, Egypt, Jordan, and Palestine that were occupied by Israel. A number of U.N. resolutions were adopted (with U.S. support and Israeli approval), reemphasizing the inadmissibility of acquisition of land by force, calling for Israeli withdrawal from occupied territories, and urging that the more needy and deserving refugees be repatriated to their former homes.*

After the 1967 war, most Arab leaders acknowledged the preeminence of the PLO as representing the Palestinians, and a quasi government was formed to deal with matters such as welfare, education, information, health, and security. In 1969 the PLO found a strong leader in Yasir Arafat, a well-educated Palestinian who was the head of al-Fatah, a guerrilla organization. As chairman, Arafat turned much of his attention to raising funds for the care and support of the refugees and inspiring worldwide contributions to their cause. At the same time, the PLO was able to establish

---

*Currently, it is estimated that there are about 9.4 million Palestinians, of whom 3.7 million live in the West Bank and Gaza, 200,000 in East Jerusalem, 1 million in Israel, and 4.5 million in other nations.

diplomatic missions in more than a hundred countries and used its observer status in the United Nations to become one of the most powerful voices in international councils. But persistent PLO attacks on Israelis continued, both within the occupied territories and from the adjacent Arab nations.

The next exodus of Palestinians was from Jordan in 1970, the result of a civil war between a powerful force of PLO militants who had settled in Jordan and King Hussein's regular forces. When the king's troops prevailed, a new flood of refugees moved from Jordan to Lebanon, where the Palestinians had a host country that was not strong enough to reject them and where the PLO was able to form a governmental organization and even an independent militia. In much of Lebanon, as had been the case in Jordan, the PLO was soon powerful enough to challenge the sovereignty of the host government itself, and its forces launched frequent attacks across the border against Israel.

These guerrilla raids brought swift Israeli retaliation, much of which fell on Lebanese civilians, who increasingly resented their troublesome guests. The country became embroiled in civil conflict, and Syrian forces moved in to restore order in June 1976 (the year I was elected president), working out an agreement to limit the PLO militia to prescribed locations and to restrict guerrilla attacks from Southern Lebanon into Israel.

\* \* \*

# Map 5

Israel
1982–2006

Mediterranean Sea

LEBANON
Tyre
Zefat
Haifa
Nazareth
Netanya
Jenin
Nablus
WEST BANK
Israeli occupied
Tel Aviv
Ramallah
Jerusalem
GAZA STRIP
Palestinian
controlled
Gaza
Rafah
Hebron
Beersheba
El Arish

ISRAEL

NEGEV

EGYPT

SINAI

Damascus
Mt. Hermon
SYRIA
GOLAN
HEIGHTS
Israeli occupied
Sea of
Galilee
Irbid
Jordan River
Amman
JORDAN
Dead
Sea
Al Karak

N
W      E
S

Israeli Settlements

0    10    20    30 miles
0   10  20  30  40 kilometers

Aqaba
Gulf of
Aqaba

SAUDI
ARABIA

*61*

I have found Palestinians in the West Bank and Gaza to be focused on their personal problems under Israeli occupation, but there are a variety of concerns among Palestinian leaders in other countries. Their attitudes and commitments have been shaped by earlier events affecting their own lives, and nowadays few have any direct contact with either the Jews or Arabs who still live in Palestine. They were driven in 1948 and 1967 from what they still consider their homes, and many I have met have claimed the right to use any means at their disposal, including armed struggle, to regain their lost rights.

When I met with Yasir Arafat in 1990, he stated, "The PLO has never advocated the annihilation of Israel. The Zionists started the 'drive the Jews into the sea' slogan and attributed it to the PLO. In 1969 we said we wanted to establish a democratic state where Jews, Christians, and Muslims can all live together. The Zionists said they do not choose to live with any people other than Jews. . . . We said to the Zionist Jews, all right, if you do not want a secular, democratic state for all of us, then we will take another route. In 1974 I said we are ready to establish our independent state in any part from which Israel will withdraw. As with Israelis, there are many differences among the voices coming from the PLO, and listeners interpret the words to suit their own ends."

When I asked Arafat about the purposes of the PLO, he seemed somewhat taken aback that I needed to ask such a question. He gave me a pamphlet that stated, "The Palestine

Liberation Organization (PLO) is the national liberation movement of the Palestinian people. It is the institutional expression of Palestinian nationhood. . . . The PLO is to the Palestinian people what other national liberation movements have been to other nations. It is their means to reassert and reaffirm a denied national identity, to recover a suppressed history, to safeguard a popular heritage, to rebuild demolished institutions, to maintain national unity threatened by physical dispersion, and to struggle for usurped homeland and denied national rights. In brief, the PLO is the Palestinian people's quest to resurrect their national existence." It is interesting how many times "national" appears in this short statement.

The PLO is a loosely associated umbrella organization bound together by common purpose, but it comprises many groups eager to use diverse means to reach their goals. The PLO has been recognized officially by all Arab governments as the "sole and legitimate representative of the Palestinian people, both at home [in Palestine] and in the Diaspora [in other nations]." It plays a strong role in the United Nations, and the many U.N. resolutions supporting Palestinians are considered to be proof of their effectiveness and the rightness of their cause.*

*The Palestine Liberation Organization is the official organization that is recognized by the international community and has observer status in the United Nations. The Palestinian National Authority was formed in 1996, with leaders elected within the occupied territories, where its jurisdiction exists.

The political prestige and influence of the Palestinians seem to increase in inverse proportion to their military defeats. After losing its effort to use Jordan as a base of operations against Israel in 1970–71, the PLO rebounded as the exclusive leader of the Palestinian people, with a strong base of operations in Lebanon. After Camp David and the Israeli-Egyptian peace treaty removed Egypt as a major supporter, the PLO seemed to gain new life as other irate Arabs renewed their commitment to the cause.

## THE ISRAELIS

One must consider the Jewish experience of the past. Jews suffered for centuries the pain of the Diaspora and persistent persecution in almost every nation in which they dwelt. Despite their remarkable contributions in all aspects of society, many Jews were killed and others driven from place to place by Christian rulers. Although not given the same rights as Muslims, both Christians and Jews who lived in Islamic countries often fared better than non-Christians in Christendom, because the Prophet Muhammad commanded his followers to recognize the common origins of their faith through Abraham, to honor their prophets, and to protect their believers. Muslim leaders favored the Jews over Christians because they saw them as less competitive in expanding their political and religious influence. President Anwar Sadat made these points often while he was negotiating with

Israeli Prime Minister Menachem Begin and me at Camp David.

Nationalism became a powerful force in nineteenth-century Europe, and it influenced Jews living there to create the Zionist movement. In Western Europe, the unique identity of the Jewish population was threatened by assimilation into Christian and secular society. But almost three-fourths of Jews were living in Eastern Europe, where persecution continued, and it was there that the seeds of Zionism were nourished. Although a majority of Jewish emigrants went to the United States in the late nineteenth and early twentieth centuries, increasing demands were heard for the establishment of a Jewish state—both to escape oppression and to fulfill an interpretation of biblical prophecies.

Although exact data are not available, it is estimated that in 1880 there were only 30,000 Jews in Palestine, scattered among 600,000 Muslim and Christian Arabs. By 1930 their numbers had grown to more than 150,000.

The Arabs in Palestine fought politically and militarily against these new settlers, but they could agree on little else and dissipated their strength and influence by contention among themselves. The British, who succeeded the Ottoman Turks after World War I as rulers of Palestine, attempted to contain the bloody disputes by restricting immigration of Jews to the Holy Land, despite desperate appeals from those who faced increasing threats and racial abuse. And then came the world's awareness of the horrors of the Holocaust, and the need to acknowledge the Zionist movement and an Israeli state.

There had been further waves of Jewish and Gentile immigration into Palestine, as indicated by official British data: the Arab population increased from 760,000 in 1931 to 1,237,000 in 1945, mostly attracted by economic opportunity, while the number of Jews during the same period increased to 608,000, primarily because of persecution in Europe.

British forces withdrew in May 1948 and Israel declared itself an independent state, recognized almost immediately by President Harry Truman on behalf of the United States. At that point Arab troops from Egypt, Lebanon, Syria, Transjordan, and Iraq joined Palestinians in attacking Israel, but their separate national forces were not well coordinated and there was some doubt about their specific objectives. The Israelis, in contrast, were cohesive, better armed, well led, and highly motivated as they fought for their lives and their new nation. The war ended in 1949 with armistice agreements signed between Israel and the proximate countries, based on Israel's acceptance of a divided Palestine (77 percent Israeli, 23 percent Arab) and the assumption that Jordan would control what is now known as East Jerusalem and the West Bank. No serious consideration was given by Arab leaders or the international community to establishing a separate Palestinian state while these people's ancient homeland was divided among Jordan, Israel, and Egypt.

The continuing state of war between Israel and its neighbors caused many Jews to flee Syria, Iraq, and other Arab countries to Israel, while Palestinian refugees were scattered more broadly. From all sides, the Palestinians and sometimes troops of their host countries launched spasmodic but persistent attacks against the Israelis, who responded with retaliatory raids. The major defining war was the one in 1967. Israel prevailed after only six days of fighting and occupied lands of Egypt and Syria and the parts of Palestine controlled by Jordan.

Of necessity, Israel has maintained one of the most powerful military forces in the world and has managed to dominate its adversaries, but none of the several wars has resolved any of the basic causes of conflict. According to official Israeli figures, about 22,000 Israelis have died in military confrontations since the nation was founded. During most engagements, the number of Arab casualties has been three or four times greater than Israeli casualties. In addition, large numbers of Christian and Muslim Arabs have either been driven into exile or put under military rule each time Israel has occupied and retained more Arab territory. This has intensified the fear, hatred, and alienation on both sides, and made more difficult the ultimate reconciliation that must come before peace, justice, and security can prevail in the region.

When I travel in the Middle East, one persistent impression is the difference in public involvement in shaping national policy. It is almost fruitless to seek free expressions of opinion from private citizens in Arab countries with more authoritarian leadership, even among business leaders, journalists, and scholars in the universities. Only among Israelis, in a democracy with almost unrestricted freedom of speech, can one hear a wide range of opinion concerning the disputes among themselves and with Palestinians, other Arabs—and often with former presidents and other distinguished guests.

When I made a presidential visit to Israel in March 1979, I was invited to address the Knesset. I was shocked by the degree of freedom permitted the members of the parliament in their exchanges. Although I was able to conclude my remarks with just a few interruptions, it was almost impossible for either Prime Minister Begin or others to speak. Instead of being embarrassed by the constant interruptions and even the physical removal of an especially offensive member from the chamber, Begin seemed to relish the verbal combat and expressed pride in the unrestrained arguments. During an especially vituperative exchange, he leaned over to me and said proudly, "This is democracy in action."

With the exception of sometimes excessive military censorship, this freedom of expression prevails in the news media, and in private discussions in Israel there is a noticeable desire to explore every facet of domestic and international political life. Only among some of the Israeli Arabs is there an obvious reluctance to speak freely.

Although important disagreements exist among opposing political leaders in the Israeli debates, the differences pale when questions of Israel's security are concerned. Then the population closes ranks. A common religion, a shared history, and memories of horrible suffering bind them together in a strength and cohesion unequaled in the Middle East or perhaps anywhere in the world.

The key to the future of Israel will not be found outside the country but within. It is not likely that any combination of Arab powers or even the powerful influence of the United States could force decisions on Israel concerning East Jerusalem, the West Bank, Palestinian rights, or the occupied territories of Syria. These judgments will be made in Jerusalem, through democratic processes involving all Israelis who can express their views and elect their leaders. The crucial issues are being debated much more vehemently there than anywhere in the outside world, and a final decision has not been made. The outcome of this debate will shape the future of Israel; it may also determine the prospects for peace in the Middle East—and perhaps the world.

# 5

## OTHER NEIGHBORS

Except for Egypt's contacts with the Palestinians, the Arab nations surrounding Israel do not now play a constructive role in any potential peace process, but their cumulative influence will be vital in helping to consummate an acceptable agreement and in assuring doubtful Israelis that such a peace can be dependable and permanent. It will be helpful to summarize the past involvement and assessments of the leaders of Syria, Jordan, Egypt, Lebanon, and Saudi Arabia concerning their potential involvement in possible solutions. I have visited these countries as often as possible and arranged for additional meetings with their leaders either in the United States or elsewhere.

### SYRIA

Israel has relinquished its control over previously occupied portions of Egypt and almost all of Lebanon but still occupies a region of Syria encompassing the Golan Heights. It is interesting to observe that when "Golan Heights" is entered into Google, one of the initial responses is an invitation to international tourists to come and visit the Israeli settlers who live there. I first visited this high plateau in 1973 and have returned to the general area several times on trips to Israel, Jordan, and Syria. Israel captured the Heights from Syria in the 1967 Six-Day War and in 1981 passed a law that seems to imply its permanent jurisdiction over the area. This is an extreme irritant in Damascus and has caused Syrian leaders to be in the forefront of Arabs who have resisted accommodation with Israel on any other issue.

When I became president, one of my primary goals was to persuade Syrian President Hafez al-Assad to change this negative policy and cooperate with me on a comprehensive peace effort. Little was known about his personal or family life, but former secretary of state Henry Kissinger and others who knew Assad had described him to me as very intelligent, eloquent, and frank in discussing even the most sensitive issues. I invited the Syrian leader to come to see me in Washington, but he replied that he had no desire ever to visit the United States. Despite this firm but polite rebuff, I learned what I could about him and his nation before meeting him.

The failure of the Arab states to destroy the new State of Israel in 1949 had aroused a wave of self-criticism among and between them, and in 1958 their search for a new approach resulted in a union between Syria and Egypt to form the United Arab Republic. After three and a half years it became obvious that Egypt's Gamal Abdel Nasser was dominating the new nation, and dissatisfied Syrian leaders dissolved the union. As minister of defense, Hafez al-Assad and other military leaders blamed politicians for the humiliating defeat in the 1967 war, and Assad subsequently refused to obey his president's orders in 1970 to support Palestinian militants who were fighting in Jordan against King Hussein. When he was condemned for this action, he seized power in a bloodless coup.

Assad had a reputation for ruthlessness toward anyone who resisted his authority and was fervent in protecting his region from outside interference and in expanding Syria's role as a dominant force in Middle East affairs. He was willing to face serious political and military confrontations rather than yield on this principle.

We first met in Switzerland in May 1977, and I found Assad as described—by far the most eloquent leader in expressing the crux of Arab beliefs regarding Israel and the prospects for peace. He seemed somewhat haughty at first but interested in my efforts to arrange peace negotiations. He insisted that peace talks had to comply with U.N. Resolutions 242 and 338 (Appendices 1 and 2) and must include the Soviets, and he objected strongly to bilateral discussions between Israel and any Arab nation and to the exclusion of the Soviet Union. Syria depended heavily on Soviet aid, but

Assad was not a subservient puppet, and I hoped that he might demonstrate his independence by working with me to overcome some of the obstacles we faced. My own plans for peace talks at that time were based on the same U.N. resolutions that he emphasized.

In order to understand the still-prevailing attitudes in the Arab world, even including the more moderate views in Egypt, Jordan, and Lebanon, it is useful to summarize the fervent opinions of Assad, which are rarely heard in the Western world. Rosalynn and I, plus official interpreters, kept careful notes of our conversations.

Assad stressed to me that Israel was admitted to the United Nations in 1949 with the clear proviso that Palestinian refugees would be allowed to return to their homeland or be fully compensated for their lost property. Prior to 1967, he said, Israel was steadily forcing additional Arab inhabitants from their small remaining territory in violation of U.N. agreements that the Israelis had sworn to honor, and he claimed that they initiated the 1967 war in order to take even more Arab land.

He quoted key Israeli leaders who had announced that this was just an intermediate step toward an ultimate "Greater Israel," and every action since that time, he said, had demonstrated their expansionist commitments. Assad was convinced that the Israelis did not want peace and would always frustrate negotiations as they expanded geographically. He emphasized that, as a matter of principle, no Arab leader could ever agree to any extension of Israel's legal borders no matter how great his desire for peace.

I tried to convince Assad that the Israelis were ready for peace if Arab leaders were willing to negotiate with them directly and in good faith. I described the overwhelming commitment of the Israelis to the security of their small nation and their need to be accepted as a permanent entity in the region. Assad pointed out that the West Bank made up only 22 percent of the British Mandate, about a fourth of what the Israelis had obtained, and he condemned their expansion into Syria's Golan Heights.

"It is strange to insist on secure borders on other people's territory. Why should their secure border be in the backyard of Damascus but quite distant from Tel Aviv?"

He added, almost as an afterthought, "We are all the time talking about religion. If Jerusalem is taken from us, we Muslims would be soulless. It is inconceivable that we should be clamoring for a return to the 1967 borders and exclude only Jerusalem."

"Would it make it any easier if we make other exclusions as well?" I asked.

He laughed along with our advisers around the conference table. "If the Israelis insist on keeping East Jerusalem, this shows that they do not want peace, because we are as attached to it as they are," he replied.

I answered that other Christians and I were deeply committed to Jerusalem and hoped that all believers would have unimpeded access to the holy shrines and the right to worship there without restraint. Before we adjourned our meeting, Assad promised to make some positive statements about the peace effort, adding that a year or two earlier it would have meant political suicide in Syria to talk about peace with the Israelis.

I asked him why Syria had never recognized Lebanon as a separate and independent nation and seemed to consider it part of Syria. Assad disavowed any designs on his western neighbor, insisting that he and his people recognized Lebanon's independence without equivocation. He claimed to prefer a free and independent Lebanon and vowed to withdraw his troops "when requested to do so by the Arab League and the Lebanese government," but it seemed obvious that he never expected this request to be made.

Assad complained that the Israelis consider it the right of every Jew in the world, needy or not, to settle in the Arab territories that they control by force while refusing to allow homeless and suffering Arabs driven out of their country to return to the dwellings and lands to which they still hold legal deeds. He argued that, while Israel claimed the right to its statehood in Palestine in 1948 because it was only recreating a nation demolished in ancient times, it rejected the recognition of a Palestinian state in the same area—the very place that generations of Palestinians, either Christian or Muslim, have inhabited continuously for thousands of years.

Furthermore, no other nation on earth, he added, including the United States, recognizes Israel's present claims for lands it has confiscated since 1949.

The Syrian leader also said that Israelis asserted that the Jews of the world constitute one people, regardless of obvious differences in their identities, languages, customs, and citizenship, but deny that the Palestinians comprise a coherent people even though they have one national identity, one language, one culture, and one history. Many Arabs consider these distinctions to be a form of racism by which Israelis regard Palestinian Arabs as inferiors who are not worthy of basic human rights, often branding them as terrorists if they resist Israel's encroachments. He scoffed at Israel's claim to be a true democracy, maintaining that its political and social equality are only for Jews.

Concerning the search for peace, Assad argued that to ensure security for themselves, Israelis create excuses to expand, to occupy new lands, and to build permanent military outposts that are developed into civilian settlements. Obviously with the Golan Heights in mind, he said that they then create circumstances to defend the new settlements by further expansion, strengthened military forces, and the displacement of the Arab inhabitants.

The loss of Arab life, he claimed, is relatively insignificant to the Israelis and their American backers, who associate all Palestinians with terrorism in an attempt to justify this racist attitude. The explanation for such a joint policy is a

United States–Israeli ambition to dominate the Middle East at the expense of its native people, who want only freedom and the right to live peaceably in their own homes. Assad explained that by refusing to discuss peace directly with the Palestinians, the United States and Israel block negotiations, except when they might single out one Arab group at a time and induce it by threats or economic blandishments to work with Israel and the United States alone.

Assad maintained that Syria had proven its willingness to work for peace in the following ways that were shared neither by Israel nor the United States:

- By honoring all U.N. resolutions concerning the Arab-Israeli conflict;

- By supporting the overwhelming international decision that the Palestinian people have, like others on earth, a right to self-determination;

- By observing international laws that prohibit the occupation and annexation of land belonging to others;

- By defining its own borders and honoring the internationally recognized borders of others; and

- By offering to withdraw Syria's forces from Lebanon when requested to do so by the Lebanese government.

Although Assad gave no indication of being willing to abandon any of his long-term objectives, I came away from our first meeting convinced that he might be sufficiently independent and flexible to modify his political tactics to accommodate changing times and circumstances. Even in his bitterness toward Israel he retained a certain wry humor about their conflicting views, seeming to derive patience from a belief that history, as during the Crusades, would be repeated in an ultimate Arab victory.

During subsequent trips to Syria, I spent hours debating with Assad and listening to his analyses of events in the Middle East. He had been furious when Sadat first told him of his planned visit to Jerusalem, and he never forgave him for his "betrayal" of the Arab cause. He saw Sadat as having been seduced by Israel into a unilateral act that would give Egypt back its lands at the expense of other Arabs. The Syrians did everything possible to prevent direct talks between Israel and Egypt or any other of its neighbors and then led an effort to isolate and boycott Egypt. Even in death Sadat was not forgiven. The streets of Damascus were filled with cheering throngs when his assassination was announced.

Assad blamed Sadat and the peace treaty with Israel for subsequent attacks on Lebanon. He maintained that the Israelis would not have taken the risk of concerted retaliation against the PLO if Egypt had been free to join forces with the other Arabs. We had heated exchanges. I would remind Assad that Egypt had its land back and its people were living in peace. I quoted passages from the Camp David Accords to prove that the framework mandated withdrawal by Israel from occupied territory, Palestinian self-determination, and a peaceful resolution of the outstanding differences between Israel and its other Arab neighbors.

After one long meeting, Assad stood in his office before a large painting depicting the battle of Hittin in 1187. In that historic engagement, the Muslim leader Saladin defeated the Christian invaders, and the Crusaders' Kingdom of Jerusalem fell. The Arabs were victorious over the West. As Assad discussed the Crusades and the other struggles for the Holy Land, he seemed to speak like a modern Saladin—as though it was his obligation to rid the region of foreign presence while preserving Damascus as the focal point for modern Arab unity.

When I met with Hafez al-Assad for the last time in 1999, at the funeral of King Hussein, he had had mixed successes. Israeli troops were almost completely out of Lebanon, but Jordan and Israel had concluded a peace treaty five years earlier. He was very frail, with only a year to live—not long enough to see his son, President Bashar al-Assad, remove all Syrian troops from Lebanon in 2005.

I made a visit to the Middle East early in 2005 and planned to visit the young Syrian president in Damascus. As usual, I notified the White House well in advance of my itinerary and immediately received a call from the national security advisor, who informed me that I would not receive approval for this portion of my trip. Because of differences with Syria concerning U.S. policy in Iraq, a decision had been made to withdraw our ambassador and to isolate President Assad by prohibiting visits by prominent Americans. I tried to explain that I had known Bashar since he was a university student and that I would be glad to use my influence to resolve any outstanding problems, as I had done with his father. In a somewhat heated conversation, I also expressed my view that refusing to communicate with leaders with whom we disagreed was counterproductive. Reluctantly, I complied with the directive. Later, I observed that President Assad was denied a visa to attend a U.N. General Assembly summit meeting in New York.

Despite this effort to embarrass and weaken Bashar al-Assad, he has survived for six years in one of the most difficult political posts in the region. It is quite likely that he has been pushed into stronger alliances with anti-American forces in Iraq, Iran, and Lebanon. When an international peace effort is launched to end the current conflict between Israel and Lebanon, Syria may once again play a major role.

## JORDAN

When Rosalynn and I first saw Jordan in the spring of 1973, we were looking through barbed wire from the West Bank at the green fields across the Jordan River. As guests of Israeli

Prime Minister Golda Meir, we were welcomed to the crossing at the Allenby Bridge, where we observed a large and uninterrupted stream of people going back and forth between the two countries. Border inspections were perfunctory, and there was almost a carnival air about the busy scene.

In 1983, after I had been president, we went back to the Allenby Bridge. Israeli uniforms were everywhere, and only a trickle of people was crossing the border. Lines extended for hundreds of yards, an uneven row of vehicles and campsites that looked as if some of the people and their produce had been waiting for days. There was a sense of tension and animosity in both directions.

This time we were traveling from Jerusalem to Amman, following weeks of skirmishing by my staff with U.S. diplomatic officials in both countries. Finally, I became the first person to make the crossing using just one passport, because if documents were stamped first in either Israel or an Arab country, they would not be honored by the other. When we reached the center of the bridge, there was no exchange of pleasantries between the stone-faced officials of the two countries.

Rosalynn and I were driven to the royal compound, on a hill near the old city. From our guesthouse we could look across a deep ravine at the bustling streets of a residential area where housing, mostly for Palestinian refugees, had been built in recent years. Some of our escort remembered that King Hussein's grandfather, King Abdullah ibn-

Hussein, enjoyed practicing long-range marksmanship at what were then unoccupied hills across the valley.

A direct descendant of the Prophet Muhammad, Abdullah had fought well against the Turks in World War I, and the British had wanted to reward him. At first he was considered for the crown of Iraq, but the British decided to give that honor to his brother Faisal. Another throne was needed, so an emirate called Transjordan was created out of some remote desert regions of the Palestine Mandate, and Abdullah had his crown, though little authority. It was not until 1946 that Transjordan was given independence, and still the British ambassador retained control over foreign policy and most financial and military matters.

Following the Arab-Israeli war of 1948, King Abdullah claimed the land on the west bank that was not part of Israel, including the old walled city of East Jerusalem, with its numerous holy shrines. The Palestinians accepted Jordan's decision, and this action was confirmed by a 1949 armistice between Abdullah and the Israelis. Transjordan became the Kingdom of Jordan and struggled to absorb almost 400,000 refugees who had lost their homes in what became the new nation of Israel. Only 6 percent of Jordan's land area was in the West Bank, but nearly two-thirds of the population and a large portion of its natural and financial resources were now Palestinian.

About a third of the Palestinians in Jordan were in camps; the others lived wherever they could find temporary shelter— in churches, mosques, tents, caves, shacks, and public buildings. Some refused to accept permanent housing, claiming that their only home was in Palestine. Many of the displaced persons remained unemployed and subsisted on food allocations from United Nations relief agencies. Even so, life in the West Bank had been relatively prosperous, so the average Palestinian was better educated, better fed, and more active politically than his East Bank neighbor. When the official merger of the West Bank with Jordan was approved by the Jordanian parliament in April 1950, all Palestinians were offered citizenship. Many participated in Jordan's political affairs, but they still retained their identity as Palestinians.

Although there were strong objections among the Arabs to acceptance of the State of Israel, King Abdullah was reported to be meeting secretly with the Israelis. He was assassinated in July 1951 by a Palestinian extremist on the Temple Mount in Jerusalem in the presence of his grandson Hussein ibn-Talal, and a little more than two years later the young man became king when he reached the age of eighteen. By this time, the Palestinians had been allotted half the parliamentary seats and the same portion of top positions in the government. The young king continued to press for Jordanian independence, and in 1956 he ordered British officials and military personnel to leave Jordan. It was to be the most popular decision of his reign.

King Hussein's greatest political disaster came in the Six-Day War of 1967, when Israeli troops occupied East Jerusalem and the entire West Bank. Jordan lost almost half its population, a major source of tourist income from the holy sites of Jerusalem and Bethlehem, and large areas of productive land. At the same time, almost 250,000 additional refugees from the West Bank settled in Jordan on the eastern side of the river.

Despite Hussein's efforts to control them, during the late 1960s the increasingly powerful Palestinians used some of the refugee camps as commando bases for their almost constant attacks on Israel. Many of these militants welcomed retaliatory raids on Jordan because one of their objectives was to weaken Hussein and replace the monarchy with a republic like that of Nasser's Egypt. By September 1970 a full-scale civil war was raging in Jordan between Hussein's armed forces and the guerrilla bands. It was at that time that Syrian Defense Minister Assad refused to attack Jordan's forces and Hussein was able to prevail. The Syrians withdrew, many Palestinians fled to Lebanon, and order was restored. Admired for his honesty and benevolence, Hussein was able to attract strong financial support from the international community, much of which was channeled to the Palestinians.

Having ascended to the throne in 1953, Hussein had become the senior national ruler on earth when we visited him, serving in the thirtieth year of his reign. His fellow world leaders respected his opinions because they were always moderate and carefully considered. Hussein had much more personal strength and influence than his weak kingdom permitted him to exhibit. He had condemned Sadat after the peace treaty between Egypt and Israel, but I was hoping he would renew diplomatic relations with Egypt and become reconciled with the Palestinians.

King Hussein made it clear that he considered the persistent unrest, instability, and tension in the region a threat to his kingdom, especially if the Palestinians could not achieve lives of peace and dignity. He was fearful that new waves of refugees might pour into Jordan because of the Israeli effort to absorb the occupied areas. He considered the inability of Palestinians to express their legitimate rights the basic cause of political ills that plagued the area.

Like Assad, the king took pride in having supported the major international proposals designed to end conflict in the region. He and almost all other Arab leaders persistently equate the plight of the Palestinians with that of the Jews following World War II—without national or individual rights, forced from their homeland, still suffering from the oppression of a military power after more than a generation. In carefully orchestrated presentations to visitors, the Jordanians claim that the constant policy of Israel is to tighten its military hold on the West Bank and Gaza, to compete with the Palestinians for the choice locations, and to make life for them as onerous as possible in order to evict the Arab population from their own land. Hussein emphasized to us that about 12,000 Palestinians a year were being induced or forced to leave their ancestral homes and move east, either into Jordan or to join the many wandering refugees in other countries.

Acknowledging that the Israeli-Egyptian treaty gave a fresh momentum to the peace process, the Jordanians maintained that the advantages were offset by the neutralization of Egypt and by Israel's increasingly domineering role in the occupied territories. During one of my later visits, the Jordanians informed me that Ronald Reagan, when he was president, had given them direct and unequivocal assurances that Israeli settlement activity would be frozen as a condition of the commencement of any expanded peace talks. They added that the Israelis rejected any political decision to cease settlement activity.

The king and his brother Crown Prince Hassan could quote the latest Israeli figures on how much Palestinian family land was being confiscated by Israel's military authorities, and they claimed that the societal structure of non-Jews was being changed methodically from family farming and free enterprise into day labor, with Palestinians becoming increasingly dependent on menial household jobs and other work for Israelis. They showed me statistics to prove that water resources from the upper Jordan River valley were being channeled almost exclusively to Israelis and that Arabs were even prohibited from digging a new well or deepening an old one dried up by adjacent wells being dug by Jewish settlers. They condemned Israel's policy of forbidding the delivery of foreign aid through Amman to the West Bank and Gaza for such projects as education, housing, and agriculture.

We had already heard most of these complaints from those living in the West Bank and Gaza, but now we were presented with color photographs, bar graphs, pages of statistics, and official documents. It was clear that Jordan's royal family was making the same presentation to other visitors and to audiences in international forums. Jordan's leaders were convinced that Israel's move "to colonize and eventually to annex" substantial portions of the occupied territories not only would change the basic character of Israel but would jeopardize her peace treaty with Egypt and friendly relations with all other neighbors. This would end all viable attempts to reach a peaceful settlement of Arab-Israeli differences and lead eventually to another broader and more deadly holy war, with Muslim forces committed through their religious beliefs to restore the rights of their Arab brothers who live west of the Jordan River or who claim the right to live there.

Even without such a conflict, many Jordanians feel that a failure to resolve the Palestinian issue may lead to the destruction of their own nation, and they listen with anger and concern to some extreme Israeli spokesmen who say, "Jordan is Palestine." This threat is real and vital to Jordan's leaders.

Following the death of King Hussein in 1999, his son Abdullah II assumed the throne, and he has seemed to continue his father's attitude of cautious idealism. Despite limits on his influence, his personal integrity and commitment to Middle East peace are acknowledged.

## EGYPT

Our family has always enjoyed visiting Egypt to cruise on the Nile, travel through the countryside, examine the ancient sites, and meet with political leaders. We still receive the warmest of welcomes, but it has not been the same for us since Sadat. Of almost a hundred heads of state with whom I met while president, he was my favorite and my closest personal friend. In fact, our wives and two other generations of our families also forged close relationships. We made a special trip to Sadat's home village after his death, to repay a visit he had made to our home in Plains.

One morning in the early 1980s, as we were approaching the entrance to the tomb of Tutankhamen, a group of Israelis saw me and began to sing *"Hayveynu Shalom Aleichem"*— "Peace Be with You." We stopped to listen, and I noticed that my eyes were not the only ones that glistened. I went over to talk to them, and they thanked me "for giving us the opportunity to visit our new friends in Egypt." I learned that 50,000 Palestinians from the occupied territories were crossing the border from Gaza into Egypt without incident, in addition to 33,000 Israeli tourists coming to Cairo and Alexandria each year. These were comparatively halcyon days, and the Israeli tourists and Egyptians we met in their homes and marketplaces were pleased and thankful for what they thought would be an era of peace and friendship.

On one trip around Egypt, in a private plane, I received

permission to depart from the normal flight paths, and we landed near Mount Sinai, where the Bible describes the Ten Commandments being delivered to Moses. We hiked up to St. Catherine's Monastery, which has huddled against the north face of the rugged mountain for more than 1,450 years—the oldest continuously occupied Christian monastery on earth. Sadat saw this "Mountain of God" as a symbol of peace and wanted a shrine for all three religions to be built there. His dream was never realized.

During many conversations with Sadat, I often expressed apprehension about Egypt's growing isolation from the other Arab nations, but he would scoff at my concern. He was certain that his bold initiative represented his own people's aspirations for peace, and he was equally convinced that most of Israel's other Arab neighbors had the same ambition, at least among the people themselves. He strongly and publicly condemned the leaders of those nations for their short-sighted timidity when they failed to follow his example.

Sadat proved to be right about the fruitlessness of attempts to punish Egypt. The other Arabs could not long exclude or ignore Egypt, with its formidable armed forces, central location, ancient cultural heritage, heterogeneous population of 47 million, large external workforce, and the willingness of its leaders to explore bold new concepts. A Tel Aviv University professor told me that the Arabs' attitude toward Egypt during their attempted boycott reminded him of an old headline in the London *Times*, "Fog in Channel. Europe Isolated."

There were repeated calls for the death of Sadat, but the Egyptian leader was not disturbed and calmly proceeded to pursue the goal of peace. After receiving the Nobel Peace Prize and even being honored in America as *Time* magazine's Man of the Year, he was assassinated on October 6, 1981. President Hosni Mubarak has been careful to honor the peace agreements of his predecessor but has concentrated more on the internal political and economic affairs of his country while working with other leaders to restore Egypt's role as a leading Arab nation.

When pressed to continue dealing favorably with their neighbor, many Egyptians ask, "Which Israel?" Increasingly concerned, they now describe the territories as being filled with "small new ghettos of Israelis armed and looking at the Arabs around them as enemies," and they see the extensive settlements as aggravating and perpetuating the hatred that Sadat believed would end with his commitment to peace. For President Mubarak and other Egyptian leaders, the vital peace treaty is always considered to be just one part of the overall Camp David agreement, with Egypt pledged to respect the entire package as long as Israel can be expected to honor the agreements concerning Palestinian rights, the withdrawal of military and political forces from the West Bank, and other specific terms of the Camp David Accords.

A final decision by Israeli leaders to retain the occupied land and a nullification of the Israeli-Egyptian Peace Treaty of 1979 would be a fatal blow to sustained peace in the region. This would bring Middle Eastern affairs back full circle—to an isolated Israel surrounded by united and implacable Arab foes, waiting patiently as they prepare someday for another opportunity to strike a fatal blow.

## LEBANON

Until the most recent outbreak of violence between Lebanon and Israel, circumstances in Lebanon had been a minor factor in the ongoing dispute between Israelis and Palestinians, but it is useful to review previous events in order to understand the causes of conflict and the potential for peace.

Lebanon has long had to accommodate religious and political divisions, with a Christian majority at the time of its formation under French control at the end of World War I and a growing Muslim influence. The mountainous terrain permitted the different religious communities to live in relative isolation and to preserve their identity and autonomy through the centuries, even while ruled by the Ottoman Empire. A constitution was evolved in 1926 under the French mandate that provided for the president to be chosen by a two-thirds vote of the National Assembly and by unwritten custom to be a Maronite Christian, with the prime minister a Sunni Muslim and the speaker of the parliament a Shia Muslim. Other government posts were divided among the Druze, Greek Orthodox, and Greek Catholics. Despite horrendous wars, political upheavals, and a present population with a growing Muslim majority, these general "confessional" political arrangements have prevailed.

Loyalty to family and religious groups transcends any commitment to national unity, and memories of injustice and past conflicts are nurtured by the wronged parties for long periods of time and have precipitated acts of retaliation and revenge. Political and religious factions have established independent militias, who have frequently depended upon foreign powers to intercede on their behalf. The Muslim Turks have favored the Druze, the French came in to protect the Maronite Christians, the Russians support the Russian Orthodox, the Syrians have on different occasions been aligned with various sides, and the Israelis and Maronites have worked closely as military allies. Members of the more militant Hezbollah have strong ties to both Iran and Syria. Few peoples in modern times have suffered as much as the Lebanese at the hands of such a diversity of foreign powers.

It was almost impossible for me to remember the different alignments in Lebanon while I was president, so I finally directed the CIA to include in weekly briefings a summary description of the political and religious organizations, their current leaders, the size and effectiveness of each militia, any foreign connections, and the latest changes in their status. Only then could I understand the news reports from the troubled country.

Lebanon's leaders have long claimed a neutral foreign policy between East and West and between Israel and Syria.

They have not always succeeded, but at least the collective Lebanese government has never mounted a threat to any of its neighbors.

A civil war erupted in 1975, with Christian forces fighting against Palestinians and other Muslims as they contended for economic and political advantage. Syrian President Assad dispatched troops into the war-torn country to restore order. This move was approved by Lebanese government officials representing all major factions, and also by Israel, the United States, and later the Arab League. Although the two countries were officially independent, Syrian leaders considered them to be "one country and one people." When I examined Syrian maps during my visits to Damascus, there was no international boundary line, and the usual bilateral diplomatic customs were not even observed between the two governments. Assad resented any implication that his troops were "invaders" or even "foreign forces" and insisted to me that he and his troops considered their presence in Lebanon to be temporary.

With Arafat as its leader, the PLO remained a strong force in Lebanon and continued cross-border attacks against Israel. In June 1982, a massive array of Israeli military forces invaded Lebanon and drove all the way to surround Beirut, with the goal of driving the PLO out of the country. The specific explanation was that the PLO had assassinated the Israeli ambassador in London, though a different group later claimed responsibility for the crime. Even as a private citizen

I was deeply troubled by this invasion, and I expressed my concern to some top Israeli leaders who had participated in the Camp David negotiations that the attack was a violation of the Accords. Back came a disturbing reply from an unimpeachable source in Jerusalem: "We had a green light from Washington." President Reagan's national security advisor denied any official approval for the invasion, but a tacit unofficial blessing was all that had been needed.*

Israel's bombing of Lebanese cities caused high civilian casualties and aroused intense opposition, even within Israel. Israel's Maronite Christian ally Bashir Gemayel was elected president of Lebanon, and under pressure from Washington, the Israelis made a partial withdrawal to the south while American and European troops entered Beirut to supervise the forced departure of Arafat and several thousand of his PLO troops. Then, in quick succession, Western peacekeeping forces left Beirut considering the crisis to be resolved, President Gemayel was assassinated, and Israeli military forces returned to the city and its suburbs. A few days later, more than a thousand non-combatant Palestinian and Lebanese Muslims were slain in the Sabra and Shatila refugee camps controlled by Israel's allies, for which Israeli Defense Minister Ariel Sharon was held accountable. American, British, French, and Italian troops moved back into Beirut.

*Current events show that history tends to repeat itself.

The Israeli forces around Beirut were under almost constant attack from Lebanese who were supported by Syria, and casualties were high. In September 1983 the Israelis again withdrew to Southern Lebanon with one of their goals accomplished: the PLO troops in Beirut and Southern Lebanon had been forced out of the area, leaving Israel's northern border more secure. American marines deployed around the Beirut airport came under increasing fire from the Lebanese militia in the surrounding hills, and U.S. forces responded with naval guns from battleships and aerial bombing from aircraft carriers offshore.

It was at this time that I made one of my visits to Lebanon, to meet with President Amin Gemayel, successor to his brother Bashir. We sat in a reception room on the top floor of the presidential palace, which had recently been bombed, and could hear and sometimes feel the tremors of distant explosions. My host did not exhibit any concern, and I pretended also to be calm. When I asked about the location of the battle, we walked out on a balcony and saw that it was concentrated in the airport area several miles away. Gemayel's main hope was that some kind of internationally monitored cease-fire might be implemented. I asked him about Assad's claim that he would withdraw Syrian troops if requested, and his quiet response was "That is the way I understand it." After a slight hesitation, he added that they would need some time to prepare for such a change.

The militant group Hezbollah ("Party of God") was

formed in Lebanon in 1982 to resist the Israeli occupation. Its members are mostly Shia Muslims, and the organization receives support from both Syria and Iran. Hezbollah is led by Hassan Nasrallah, a disciple of Iran's Ayatollah Khomeini, who led the Iranian revolution against the Shah. About 700 hardcore militia are able to expand to as many as 20,000 during times of emergency. It is a tightly knit and effective fighting force that dominates portions of Lebanon, much too strong to be controlled by the regular military forces of the nation. The civilian wing is widely respected in Lebanon for providing humanitarian services, and its political candidates hold 14 of the 128 seats in parliament. Amal, a sister Shia group, has 15 seats. In the 2005 election, these two groups won 80 percent of the votes cast in Southern Lebanon.

In April 1983, a month after my visit to Beirut, 63 people were killed by a bomb at the American embassy, and later a deadly explosion took the lives of 241 U.S. marines in their barracks. These attacks, combined with the shooting down of American naval planes by militia in the hills surrounding Beirut, aroused strong American political opposition to our presence in Lebanon, and U.S. troops were quickly withdrawn. This seemed to leave Assad "king of the mountain." He proclaimed that the Arabs had just won their most important victory over the United States. All Lebanese groups would now have to turn to Syria.

With American approval, Israel maintained a strong military presence in Southern Lebanon in an apparently fruitless attempt to destroy the military capability of Hezbollah. In April 1996 Israel attacked a well-known United Nations outpost at Qana, which was housing a group of 800 Lebanese who had taken cover there. More than 100 civilians were killed, and an international outcry about Lebanese casualties plus the attrition of its own military forces were major factors in Israel's decision in May 2000 to withdraw almost completely from Lebanon after eighteen years of occupation, retaining its presence only in Shebaa Farms.

Although the Lebanese have not been strong enough to defend themselves, their nation has proven resilient. Their dream has been to become something like a Switzerland in the Middle East, neither involved in conflict nor a staging area for other combatants, and benefiting from good relations with all other nations. Their government's primary complaint is that Israel holds a number of Lebanese prisoners and still occupies an area near the borders of Israel, Lebanon, and Syria known as Shebaa Farms, which Lebanon claims as its territory. Israel insists it is part of Syria, which would justify the occupation.

This is a key issue and needs to be understood. Since 1924, Shebaa Farms had been treated as Lebanese territory, but Syria seized the area in the 1950s and retained control until Israel occupied the Farms—along with the Golan Heights—in 1967. The inhabitants and properties were Lebanese, and Lebanon has never accepted Syria's control of the Farms. Although Syria has claimed the area in the past,

Syrian officials now state that it is part of Lebanon. This position supports the Arab claim that Israel still occupies Lebanese territory.

The withdrawal of all other foreign troops increased international pressure for the same action by Syria, and in 2004 the U.N. Security Council passed Resolution 1559 supporting this goal and calling for Hezbollah and other militant groups to disarm. This encouraged domestic pressures against Syria, which may have precipitated the assassination of former Prime Minister Rafiq Hariri, a Sunni Muslim, and twenty others in February 2005. Although Syria denied responsibility for the crime, Hariri was known to be a strong critic of Syrian decisions concerning the Lebanese government. Massive demonstrations followed, and Syria withdrew the remainder of its military forces. The slain prime minister's son Saad was elected to head the government. To the relief of many, Lebanon was no longer on center stage, and the light of world attention could be focused elsewhere in the Middle East. These dreams were to be shattered in July 2006, as will be described in Chapter 16.

## SAUDI ARABIA

Although not contiguous to Israel, Saudi Arabia will play an important role in any permanent peace agreement in the region. Because it is a rich nation with major oil reserves, keeper of the Muslim holy places, with diplomatic ties to almost all other nations and playing a preeminent role in the Arab League, its stabilizing influence has always been crucial. As president I had strong but private encouragement from Saudi leaders for my peace initiatives, even when their public statements were quite different.

Saudi Arabia is a strange country to many Westerners, reminiscent of the *Arabian Nights*, geographically isolated, ruled by hundreds of princes who are floating in wealth, and having enjoyed a close political relationship with the United States since the time of King Abdul Aziz and President Franklin D. Roosevelt.

Although we found the major cities very interesting, Rosalynn and I had our most informative visit with King Fahd ibn Abd in 1983 while he was having one of the customary royal sessions with his subjects, this time in a remote desert area about two hundred kilometers north of Riyadh. In a tent city erected for this purpose, chieftains had assembled to meet with their monarch, to report on their tribal affairs and to request goods and services for their people. While I was with the men, Rosalynn was whisked off to visit Saudi women, who were in a different camp entirely, over the sand dunes and out of sight. I had known Fahd for several years and, while president, had consulted with in him in both Washington and Saudi Arabia. Then he had been a most powerful crown prince, with many international duties assigned to him by his half brother King Khalid.

The monarchs maintained political stability within the

kingdom and greatly enhanced their leadership role by minimizing internal differences through close consultation, by carefully dispensing part of the nation's oil income, and by capitalizing on their preeminence as custodians of the holy places of Islam. They balanced their absolute authority with an impressive closeness to their subjects. King Khalid told me on my first visit to Saudi Arabia that each day he opened his doors to many dozens of men who wished to see him, and each week women of the families were permitted to bring their problems and requests directly to him. He traveled widely through the desert kingdom with a fleet of tractor-trailers carrying a complete mobile hospital and personally welcomed those who needed medical treatment. When I expressed concern about the time-consuming extent of these administrative chores, he replied that the kingdom could not survive if its leaders abandoned this commitment of personal service to their people.

A preeminent desire of Saudis is stability in the region. One of their prime commitments is to maintain a sense of brotherhood among Arabs, particularly with the Palestinians, whom they consider to be severely victimized, and they look upon the Palestinian-Israeli conflict as one of the most serious obstacles to permanent peace in the region. There is no doubt that Saudi leaders share Arab feelings of resentment toward the encroachment of Israel on land that was previously occupied and ruled by their Muslim brothers, but Saudi kings have expressed their support for resolving the ongoing conflict through peaceful negotiations if the results will not jeopardize the fundamental rights of the Palestinians. The Saudis consider Crown Prince (now King) Abdullah's proposal adopted by the Arab League in March 2002 (Appendix 6) to be quite compatible with the International Quartet's Roadmap for Peace,* recognizing Israel within its pre-1967 borders.

Many of us fail to recognize that, with all their wealth and prestige, the Saudis' caution in dealing with controversial issues is justified. They have a relatively small native population, their military power is limited, and they are surrounded by potentially dangerous neighbors. Their leadership is predicated on compromise and the forging of a consensus among independent and volatile leaders in a divided Arab world. I might add that the Saudis and many others greatly overestimate the influence of the United States, and they never understand why we cannot "deliver" our own friends in the Middle East when it suits our purposes.

The leaders of Saudi Arabia can be a crucial and beneficial force in the Middle East whenever their influence might make the difference in bringing peace and stability to the region as an alternative to war and continuing political turmoil. At least among American political leaders, there has been a willingness to overlook in Saudi Arabia serious human rights violations that we would condemn in other nations.

*The Quartet includes the United States, Russia, the United Nations, and the European Union and has published a plan for resolving the dispute between Israel and the Palestinians.

# 6

## THE REAGAN YEARS, 1981–89

In addition to my involvement while president, I observed very carefully the developments in the Middle East during the following years and visited the region several times to consult with political leaders, academics, and private citizens. These activities were part of the programs of The Carter Center, an organization that my wife, Rosalynn, and I founded to address issues that we considered to be important to our own country and to others. Our center now has projects in sixty-five nations, including thirty-five in Africa, dealing with health, agriculture, the enhancement of democracy, and the promotion of peace.

In the Holy Land, I found that the situation was changing dramatically. Within a few months after I left the White House, the Israelis launched an air strike that destroyed an Iraqi nuclear reactor, announced the "annexation" of the

Golan Heights, and escalated their efforts to build Israeli settlements throughout the West Bank and Gaza. All these acts were widely condemned in the Arab world, and the Israeli people were divided over the wisdom of this militant policy.

The Israelis invaded Lebanon in 1982, and within a year the PLO and its leaders had been forced to leave the country. For the next decade, the members of the organization were dispersed in many Arab nations, while they continued to build diplomatic ties throughout the world and again emerged as the sole remaining political symbol for Palestinian self-determination.

There was little effort by the United States to promote an overall peace agreement, but President Reagan, who wanted to make a clear declaration of his policy in the Middle East, called to ask if I would work with his assistants on it. His statement would include his complete support for the implementation of the Camp David Accords, and I was pleased to assist with the following portion of the speech:

We base our approach squarely on the principle that the Arab-Israeli conflict should be resolved through negotiations involving an exchange of territory for peace. This exchange is enshrined in United Nations Security Council Resolution 242, which is, in turn, incorporated in all its parts in the Camp David agreements. U.N. Resolution 242 remains wholly valid as the foundation stone of America's Middle East peace effort.

It is the United States' position that—in return for peace—the withdrawal provision of Resolution 242 applies to all fronts, including the West Bank and Gaza.

President Reagan knew that the Middle East could be stable only if Israel could have lasting peace with her neighbors and that this would not be possible if the occupied territories were retained and colonized.

Our team at The Carter Center continued to monitor the interrelated events in the Middle East, always with the goal of keeping alive the faltering peace process. Two events discouraged any strong and sustained Middle East peace efforts by the United States. In 1986, leaders in Washington were embarrassed when it was disclosed that Israeli intermediaries had assisted the United States in exchanging weapons to Iran for the release of U.S. hostages being held in Lebanon, with proceeds from the arms sales used to support the Contra war in Nicaragua. And late in 1987 the Likud settlement policy in the occupied territories increased confrontations between Jews and Arabs, and harsher treatment of dissidents led to an outbreak of organized civil violence. Known as the *intifada*, this sustained, independent, and forceful action of young Palestinians surprised both the Israelis and the PLO.

My first visit to Israel after leaving the White House illustrates how circumstances and attitudes had changed since I went there as governor ten years earlier and as president in the late 1970s. On arriving in Jerusalem in the spring of 1983, Rosalynn and I paid our third visit to the Yad Vashem Holocaust memorial, where we heard expressions of gratitude that the negotiations at Camp David had led to peace with Egypt. A few minutes later I was on my way to Prime Minister Begin's office in Israel's parliament building.

As a private citizen, I expected that my personal relationship with Israeli leaders and especially with Prime Minister Begin would be different. Although his nation and mine shared many beliefs and political goals, he and I had frequently been at odds across the negotiating table. It was no secret that Begin and I had strong public disagreements concerning the interpretation of the Camp David Accords and Israel's recent invasion of Lebanon. Unfortunately, these disputes had resulted in some personal differences as well.

Now we were together again, and as had always been my custom, I expressed myself with frankness on some of the more controversial issues. I first congratulated Begin on the manner in which he had honored the difficult terms of the peace treaty concerning the withdrawal of Israeli forces and dismantling of settlements in Egypt's Sinai. Then, as he sat without looking at me, I explained again why we believed he had not honored a commitment made during the peace negotiations to withdraw Israeli forces and to refrain from building new Israeli settlements in the West Bank. I described my disappointment that he had not been willing to grant the Palestinians any appreciable degree of independence or responsibility in the occupied territories, and I urged him to make it plain to the Egyptians and Jordanians that Israel would observe the basic elements of U.N. Resolution 242—crucial commitments that he and I had made to our people.

I paused, expecting the prime minister to give his usual strong explanation of Israeli policy. He responded with just a few words in a surprisingly perfunctory manner and made it plain that our conversation should be concluded. I did not know whether I had aggravated him more than usual, whether he wanted to reserve his arguments for current American officials, or whether he was preoccupied. Most likely, it was a combination of all three reasons.

We had been sitting in a small, sparsely adorned room on the lower level of the Knesset building. The exchanges had been cool, distant, and nonproductive. As I left, I noticed that the adjacent room was large, brightly lighted, attractive, and vacant. Ironically, the number on the door was 242.

Rosalynn and I spent several days in Israel and the occupied territories, meeting with leaders and private citizens. It was very different from the place we had first come to know ten years earlier. The sense of unanimity among Jewish citizens and the relaxed confidence of 1973 were gone. Despite their military triumph in Lebanon, many Israelis were deeply concerned that the flame of victory had turned to ashes. Military superiority that was crucial for the defense of the nation was not adequate for Israel to subdue its neighbors. The successes had been very costly in both financial and human terms, and after each war and a brief interlude of peace, both sides had plunged into a new round of violence.

Men and women in uniform were now seen everywhere, and the tension between different kinds of people was obvious. The former stream of visitors from Jordan had dried to a trickle, and visits from Egypt were almost nonexistent despite the peace treaty that had established open borders and free trade. Even among the most optimistic public officials, there seemed to be little hope for any permanent agreement that could bring peace and stability. In fact, with some justification, the Israelis were increasingly skeptical about the attitudes of all foreign governments. There were sharp differences between the policies of the United States and Israel, as demonstrated vividly by Israel's peremptory rejection of peace proposals made by Secretary of State George Shultz and President Reagan's recent speech endorsing our nation's undeviating Middle East policy that presumed Israel's withdrawal from occupied territories.

Speaking officially for the Likud coalition, for instance, Foreign Minister Yitzhak Shamir expressed his belief that the root of the Middle East conflict had nothing to do with Israel and that a solution of the Arab-Israeli conflict was not likely to affect regional stability. He minimized the importance of the Palestinian problem and considered Jews to be the natural rulers of Israel, the West Bank, and Gaza, with a right and obligation to continue populating the area. The proper homeland for Palestinian Arabs was to be found in Jordan, and the pre-1967 borders of Israel were of no consequence. Ariel Sharon went further, having called for the overthrow of King Hussein in favor of a Palestinian regime in Jordan, even if headed by Yasir Arafat. He added that the east bank of the Jordan is "ours but not in our hands, just as East Jerusalem had been until the Six-Day War."

Although they continued to state officially that any peace talks should take place within the Camp David framework, most members of Begin's ruling Likud Party never approved the concessions he had made during the intense negotiations with President Sadat and me. Both Israel and Egypt had honored the terms of the peace treaty involving the Sinai, but the original substance of the Accords relating to the other occupied territories had been abandoned or modified in vital ways. Former Israeli foreign minister Abba Eban remarked, "Unfortunately, it is clear that Israeli governmental policy is so distant from Camp David that when Likud spokesmen invoke the agreement, they are rather like Casanova invoking the Seventh Commandment."

My primary contact in Israel was Ezer Weizman, and we enjoyed frequent telephone conversations and personal visits. When we visited their beautiful home overlooking the bay in the ancient Roman city of Caesarea Maritima, Ezer and his wife, Reuma, invited a few of their neighbors to meet us, partially to demonstrate how far some of the highly educated and relatively wealthy Israelis had deliberately removed themselves from the situation involving Palestinians in the West Bank. He had been expelled from the Likud Party because of his unrestrained condemnation of the party's violations of the peace accords that he had helped to negotiate and was contemplating the formation of a new party to be led by him, Moshe Dayan, and others who had participated with us at Camp David. Remarkably outspoken and independent of any political restraints, Weizman aroused strong animosities and admiration, and in 1993 he was elected president of Israel. Until his death, he remained my closest personal friend in the Holy Land and an invaluable source of information and advice.

In addition to an estimated hundred thousand people who had died in the various wars between Israel and her neighbors, large numbers of Christian and Muslim Arabs were either displaced from their homes or put under military rule as more and more of their territory was occupied and retained. This forced relocation intensified the fear, hatred, and alienation on both sides and made more difficult any reconciliation. None of the wars had resolved either of the two basic causes of continuing conflict: land and Palestinian rights.

While on this visit to Jerusalem, I also had a personal taste of how the Israeli-Palestinian relationships had changed since my earlier tours. As usual, I got up quite early and began a jog around the old city, in East Jerusalem and beyond—an intriguing route of ancient sites and steep hills. I was accompanied by an American Secret Service agent and two young Israeli soldiers, who insisted on leading the way. We proceeded from our hotel to the Jaffa Gate, then turned north around the outside of the ancient walls. As we were running eastward alongside the Jericho road, I saw a group of elderly Arab men sitting by the curb, reading their newspapers. The sidewalk was almost empty and wide enough for us to pass easily, but one of the soldiers cut to the right and knocked all of the newspapers back into the faces of the startled readers. Some of the papers fluttered to the ground. I stopped to apologize to the old men, but they could not understand me. Then I told the soldiers either to let me run alone or not to treat anyone else in a belligerent manner. They reluctantly agreed, insisting that one could never tell what was being hidden behind newspapers. This was a sharp demonstration of our different perspectives.

The domestic political debates among Israelis were more vitriolic than I had previously observed, and it was uncertain what kind of government the people preferred. Even those who were most willing to end the military occupation, grant the Palestinians basic rights of citizenship, honor the terms of U.N. Resolution 242 and the Camp David Accords, and commence negotiations without patently unacceptable conditions were hard put to detect any reliable signs of encouragement from leaders in the Arab-Palestinian camp. Some leaders in Israel and in Arab countries expressed concern that during recent years America's policy in the Middle East had consisted of a series of illogical flip-flops, with a lack of resolve to enforce agreements that had been consummated.

It became increasingly clear that there were two Israels. One encompassed the ancient culture and moral values of the Jewish people, defined by the Hebrew Scriptures with which I had been familiar since childhood and representing the young nation that most Americans envisioned. The other existed within the occupied Palestinian territories, with policies shaped by a refusal to acknowledge and respect the basic human rights of the citizens. Even the more optimistic believed that militants would inevitably become more active on both sides, as settlements expanded and Jews and Arabs struggled for the same hilltops, pastures, fields, and water.

# 7

## MY VISITS
## WITH PALESTINIANS

During my fairly regular visits to the Middle East in the first ten years after leaving the White House, I especially wanted to learn more about the Palestinian people—how they were living, what concerned them, how they reacted to existence under a prolonged political and military occupation, and what they might propose as a peaceful relationship with Israel. I sought out a representative sample of diverse voices. In Cairo, Amman, Riyadh, Beirut, Damascus, Rabat, and among scholars in America, I listened to their perspectives on the Middle East conflict as it related to them and the refugees for whom they claimed responsibility.

Although I had publicly called for the Palestinians to have their own homeland just a few weeks after becoming president and had promoted the legal and political status of the Palestinians during the Camp David negotiations, it was during these later trips that Rosalynn and I first visited extensively among Palestinian political leaders and private families in the occupied territories. Our primary contact was through the Orient House, the official PLO office in Jerusalem, where I received information and advice from Faisal Husseini, Hanan Ashrawi, and Mubarak Awad, the latter a Palestinian Christian dedicated to nonviolence. United States diplomats also cooperated in scheduling meetings and arranging our itinerary. In the West Bank and Gaza, we spent as much time as possible with Palestinians in all walks of life in large and small communities and in the rural areas. Some of the most eloquent were lawyers who were active in defending the rights of their neighbors in the Israeli military tribunals, some were university professors, and quite a number were farmers or villagers. All wanted to describe their circumscribed life in the occupied territories.

Most of the Palestinians were Muslims but a surprising number were Christians, and I talked with many priests and pastors about their ministry. They were disturbed by the violence around them and the political and economic pressures exerted by government leaders, representing the very conservative Israeli religious parties, which were granted almost exclusive control over all forms of worship.

Our meetings took place in private homes, municipal offices, hospitals, vacant classrooms, the backs of shops or stores, and churches and mosques. In almost every case, those who agreed to meet with us had arranged to have a few family members or friends present. Before more serious discussions, we sipped black coffee, tea, or Coke and nibbled on sugary candy or cookies, talking about the weather or my general impressions of the area. At first there would be considerable reticence about broaching any subject that was sharply focused or controversial, but soon the constraints would be dropped and a more lively discussion would develop, often with bystanders and even children participating. In the larger meetings, usually several people could speak both English and Arabic and sometimes competed as translators.

On the advice of U.S. officials, we invited some special groups who were acknowledged Palestinian leaders to meet with me in Jerusalem at the American consulate, where our nation's relations with the West Bank were managed. These sessions were more formal but no less revealing. The participants presented their views as lawyers would write a brief: carefully, constructively, conclusively—often with documents to prove their case.

In all the meetings, I tried to present my own views about the need for an end to violence and better communication among the Palestinians, Israelis, and the people of the United States. My description of the Camp David agreements and basic American policy concerning the Palestinians seemed to be news to many of them, and it was obvious that their acceptance of any of these proposals would depend heavily on the PLO's interpretation. Some of them expressed hope that Arafat would approve.

These kinds of issues regarding a general peace agreement were a minor portion of the discussions. What the Palestinians wanted was to catalogue their current grievances. On one visit to Gaza, we were guests of a prominent family that was involved in agriculture, business, and international trade. We learned that after one of their sons recently had made a statement critical of the Israeli occupation, five of the father's truckloads of oranges had been held up at the Allenby Bridge crossing into Jordan for several days—until the fruit had rotted. This was a large portion of their total crop for the year. The father showed us the partly unloaded trucks and said that he was trying to give away the spoiled oranges for livestock feed.

Some showed us the wreckage of their former homes, which had been demolished by Israeli bulldozers and dynamite, with claims by Israel that they had been built too near Israeli settlements, on property needed by the Israeli government, or that some member of the family was a security threat.

In assessing these claims, the Israeli human rights organization B'Tselem explained that, on average, twelve innocent families lost their homes for every person accused of participation in attacks against Israelis, with almost half of the demolished homes never occupied by anyone suspected of involvement in any violent act against Israel, even throwing stones.

Contrary to the Israeli Defense Forces' argument before

the Supreme Court that prior warning was given except in extraordinary cases, B'Tselem's figures indicated that this warning was given in fewer than 3 percent of the cases. In addition to punitive demolitions, Israel had razed even more Palestinian homes in "clearing" operations, plus houses that Israel claimed were built without a permit. All of this destruction was on Palestinian land. B'Tselem concluded: "Israel's policy of punitive demolitions constitutes a grave breach of international humanitarian law, and therefore a war crime. Through a variety of legal gymnastics, Israel's High Court of Justice has avoided judicial scrutiny of the issue, serving as a rubber stamp for Israel's illegal policy."

Rosalynn visited the largest hospital in Gaza, and the doctors told her that they had great difficulty providing transportation for critically ill patients. They showed her a row of ambulances that had been contributed by a European nation and said that they couldn't be used. He claimed that Israeli officials refused to issue license plates because the chassis were twelve inches too long. When Rosalynn reported this to me, I promised to intercede with Israeli officials when I returned to Jerusalem. My concerns were dismissed by an explanation that there were serious security threats because of contraband crossing to and from Gaza, and tight control was required over the dimensions of all vehicles. The Palestinians couldn't be given special permits to operate even ambulances that deviated from standards set by the local military officers.

Many Palestinians emphasized that they were deprived of their most basic human rights. They could not assemble peacefully, travel without restrictions, or own property without fear of its being confiscated by a multitude of legal ruses. As a people, they were branded by Israeli officials as terrorists, and even minor expressions of displeasure brought the most severe punishment from the military authorities. They claimed that their people were arrested and held without trial for extended periods, some tortured in attempts to force confessions, a number executed, and their trials often held with their accusers acting as judges. Their own lawyers were not permitted to defend them in the Israeli courts, and appeals were costly, long delayed, and usually fruitless.

They claimed that any demonstration against Israeli abuses resulted in mass arrests of Palestinians, including children throwing stones, bystanders who were not involved, families of protesters, and those known to make disparaging statements about the occupation. Once incarcerated, they had little hope for a fair trial and often had no access to their families or legal counsel. If they were presented with charges, the alleged crimes were usually described in very general terms equivalent to "disturbing the peace," and the sentences were often indefinite. Most of the cases were tried in military tribunals, but 90 percent of the inmates were being held in civilian jails. They pointed out that this policy of holding thousands of prisoners touched almost every Palestinian family and was a major source of festering resentment.

I urged them to take the strongest test cases to the Israeli Supreme Court and tried to assure them that they would get a fair hearing and perhaps set precedents that would be beneficial in similar cases. One of the attorneys responded strongly: "At great expense we have tried this. It just does not work. It is not like the American system, where one ruling in the top courts is followed closely by all the subordinate courts. Here there is one system under civil judges and another under the military. Most of our cases, no matter what the subject might be, fall under the military. They are our accusers, judges, and juries, and they all seem the same to us. When a rare civilian court decision is made in our favor, to protect a small parcel of land, for instance, it is not looked on as a precedent. By administrative decision or decree a new procedure is born to accomplish the same Israeli goals in a different fashion. Besides," he added, "we cannot take our client's case out of the West Bank into an Israeli court. We are not permitted to practice there."

I asked, "Then why don't you employ an Israeli lawyer?"

He responded, "Sometimes we do, but few of them will take our cases. Those who will do so are heavily overworked with their own Arab clients who live in Israel. One or two Jewish members of the Knesset have tried to be helpful— mostly the most liberal members."

With the exception of Arabs who were selected by the Israelis to handle bureaucratic duties and dispense political patronage, the Palestinians we met were strong supporters of the PLO. Only rarely did anyone directly criticize the PLO, but one Palestinian attorney did complain that Arafat—they always called him Abu Ammar—and other PLO leaders "are more concerned with struggles for political power and money than with the plight of Palestinians living under the military occupation." Their primary condemnation was divided almost equally between Israel and the United States. They denounced our country for financing the Israeli settlements in the occupied territories and for supporting military actions against Arab countries.

There was a unanimous complaint among Palestinian political leaders and others that the worst and most persistent case of abuse was in Hebron, about twenty miles south of Jerusalem, where the biblical patriarchs Abraham, Isaac, and Jacob are buried. About 450 extremely militant Jews have moved into the heart of the ancient part of the city, protected by several thousand Israeli troops. Heavily armed, these settlers attempt to drive the Palestinians away from the holy sites, often beating those they consider to be "trespassers," expanding their area by confiscating adjacent homes, and deliberately creating physical confrontations. When this occurs, the troops impose long curfews on the 150,000 Palestinian citizens of Hebron, prohibiting them from leaving their own homes to go to school or shops or to participate in the normal life of an urban community. The Palestinians claimed that the undisguised purpose of the harassment was to drive non-Jews from the area. The United

Nations reported that more than 150 Israeli checkpoints had been established in and around the city.

These Palestinians were convinced that some Israeli political leaders were trying through harassment to force a much broader exodus of Muslims and Christians from the occupied territories. They claimed that any manufactured goods or farm products were not permitted to be sold in Israel if they competed with Israeli produce, so any surplus had to be given away, dumped, or exported to Jordan. The fruit, flowers, and perishable vegetables of the more activist families were often held at the Allenby Bridge until they spoiled, and in some areas the farmers were not permitted to replace fruit trees that died in their orchards. Their most anguished complaints were about many thousands of ancient olive trees that were being cut down by the Israelis. Access to water was a persistent issue. Each Israeli settler uses five times as much water as a Palestinian neighbor, who must pay four times as much per gallon. They showed us photographs of Israeli swimming pools adjacent to Palestinian villages where drinking water had to be hauled in on tanker trucks and dispensed by the bucketful. Most of the hilltop settlements are on small areas of land, so untreated sewage is discharged into the surrounding fields and villages.

Teachers and parents maintained that their schools and universities were frequently closed, educators arrested, bookstores padlocked, library books censored, and students left on the streets or at home for extended periods of time without jobs. They claimed that any serious altercation between these idle and angry young people and the military authorities could result in the sending of bulldozers into the community to destroy homes. Predictably, the Palestinians professed to deplore all acts of violence and claimed that militant Israeli settlers were as guilty as any Arabs in initiating attacks but were seldom if ever arrested or punished.

One of their most bitter grievances was that foreign aid from Arab countries and even funds sent by the American government for humanitarian purposes were intercepted by the authorities and used for the benefit of the Israelis, including the construction of settlements in Palestinian communities. They claimed that the government had seized U.S. Agency for International Development funds intended for a center for retarded children in Gaza and that Jordanian and other Arab money intended for education and the development of a poultry industry in some of the poorer communities in the West Bank was being withheld.

I was disturbed by these reports and wanted to determine if they were accurate and, if so, to hear an explanation from the Israeli authorities. Before leaving Israel, I met at length with our own diplomatic officials in Tel Aviv and Jerusalem and with Israelis who administered affairs in the occupied territories. From the Israeli point of view, life under a military occupation was inevitably going to be different from that in a free democracy, and severe restrictions were considered necessary to forestall acts of violence.

As far as the harassment of activists was concerned, I was told that there were often extended delays at the Allenby Bridge entering Jordan, but these were not designed to punish any particular families. This situation was the inevitable result of constraints on commercial traffic between two countries that did not have normal trade or diplomatic relations. Lists were kept of troublemakers, and shipments from their families received more intense inspection that sometimes resulted in their spoilage. Also, it was true that Israeli products of all kinds had first priority for sales throughout the territory. Israeli officials said that the destruction of an Arab home with dynamite or bulldozers was a rare, deliberate, and highly publicized event, designed to serve as an effective deterrent to adults who might permit or encourage illegal acts by younger members of their families.

Most of the Israeli responses were forthright, but one exception was the interception of foreign aid money by the Israelis, who claimed that some of the confiscated funds might have been diverted to finance acts of Arab terrorism and that Israeli control must be sufficient to prevent abuses that could threaten the peace. They also acknowledged a concern about surplus chickens, oranges, flowers, grapes, olives, or other agricultural goods being produced in the West Bank and Gaza that might damage the Israeli farm economy. It did not make sense for foreign money to be used to increase such agricultural production. I was told that some USAID funds appropriated by the U.S. Congress even for benevolent projects were kept by the Israeli government when necessary to prevent misspending but that this withheld money was not used to build Israeli settlements in the occupied territory.

The Israelis told me that in every instance there was a legal basis for the taking of land—or that it was needed for security purposes. In some key cases, "administrative definitions" had served to circumvent or modify legal decisions. Later I received a briefing from Meron Benvenisti, an Israeli who had served as deputy mayor of Jerusalem and was devoting his full time to a definitive analysis of Israel's policies in the occupied territories. With maps and charts, he explained that the Israelis acquired Palestinian lands in a number of different ways: by direct purchase; through seizure "for security purposes for the duration of the occupation"; by claiming state control of areas formerly held by the Jordanian government; by "taking" under some carefully selected Arabic customs or ancient laws; and by claiming as state land all that was not cultivated or specifically registered as owned by a Palestinian family. Since lack of cultivation or use for farming is one of the criteria for claiming state land, it became official policy in 1983 to prohibit, under penalty of imprisonment, any grazing or the planting of trees or crops in these areas by Palestinians. Large areas taken for "security" reasons became civilian settlements. These were apparently the sources of some of the complaints I had heard.

No legal cases concerning these land matters were permitted in the Palestinian courts; they now had to be decided by the Israeli civil governor. Since 1980, with the Likud Party in control of the government, the taking of Arab land had been greatly accelerated, and the building of Jewish settlements in the West Bank had become one of the government's top priorities. Benvenisti added that the number of Israeli settlers in the West Bank had been previously limited but that new policies and present trends meant that the further annexation of substantial occupied areas was probably a foregone conclusion. It was true that Palestinian lawyers were not permitted to practice in the Israeli courts, where most of the land issues were resolved, but he assured me that Israeli lawyers were available to represent some of the Palestinians. Most frequently, one of the more radical members of the Knesset was cited as an example.

I arranged to meet with Aharon Barak, who was one of the heroes at Camp David and later had become chief justice of the Israeli Supreme Court. We met in a hotel bar, and I began to go down a list of concerns about the maltreatment of Palestinians, referring to the orange trucks and ambulances. Barak quickly pointed out that it was not legally appropriate for him to discuss specific cases, but he explained that the judiciary had to walk a tight line between what was appropriate under the special circumstances of a military occupation and protecting the rights of people in the West Bank and Gaza. Also, the courts could deal only with cases brought before them. He admitted that it was not easy for aggrieved Palestinians to find their way through this tortuous legal path but said that the Supreme Court had always attempted to provide justice in civilian cases under its purview.

I asked the chief justice if he considered the treatment of the Palestinians to be fair, and he replied that he dealt fairly with every case brought before him in the high court but he did not have the power to initiate legal action. I asked him if he felt a responsibility to investigate the overall situation, and he replied that he had all he could do in deciding individual matters that were brought before the court. Barak said that there were special legal provisions related to the occupied territories and acknowledged that many of the more sensitive issues were turned over to military courts. When I requested his personal assessment of the situation in the West Bank and Gaza, he said that he had not been in the area for many years and had no plans to visit there. I remarked that if he was to make decisions that affected the lives of people in the occupied areas, he should know more about how they lived. He answered with a smile, "I am a judge, not an investigator."

On one of my later visits to Jerusalem, in 1990, some of the Christian leaders asked for an urgent meeting with me, but I declined because all my remaining time was scheduled. When they persisted, I finally responded that I could meet with them one evening, but only after I had finished my last engagement. At this late hour, after midnight, I was surprised to receive custodians of the Christian holy places plus cardinals, archbishops, patriarchs, and other leaders of the

Greek Orthodox, Roman Catholic, Armenian, Coptic, Ethiopian Orthodox, Maronite, Anglican, Lutheran, Baptist, and other faiths. They were distressed by what they considered to be increasing abuse and unwarranted constraints imposed on them by the Israeli government, and each of them related events that caused him concern.

Subsequently, when I met with Prime Minister Yitzhak Shamir, he assured me that there was no official inclination to discriminate against Christians. He went on to explain that the formation of a majority governing coalition required support of the smaller deeply religious parties, and their primary demands were that they be excused from military service, receive special funding for their benevolent causes, and have authority over all religious matters. He seemed to consider these matters out of his hands, and I understood for the first time why there was such a surprising exodus of Christians from the Holy Land.

# 8

---◆---

# THE
# GEORGE H. W. BUSH
# YEARS

Peace prospects seemed to improve in July 1988, when King Hussein decided to reduce Jordan's administrative role in the West Bank, and Yasir Arafat announced that the PLO would accept several United Nations resolutions that recognized Israel's right to exist within its 1967 borders. Arafat publicly disavowed terrorism as a means to achieve PLO goals and agreed that, with the formation of an independent Palestinian state, normal relations with Israel would be acceptable. Based on these statements, United States diplomats began exploratory talks with PLO officials.

The glasnost policies of Soviet President Mikhail Gorbachev helped to end the Cold War, making it possible for the two superpowers to cooperate, and at the same time, Syria and other Arab nations lost their strong political and military support from Moscow and became more willing to ease tensions in the region. Arab leaders accepted Egypt back into the Arab League in May 1989, and that same year the USSR permitted hundreds of thousands of Soviet Jews to emigrate to Israel.

Secretary of State James Baker understood the need to ease tension in the Middle East and in May 1990 stated to the annual convention of the powerful pro-Israeli lobbying organization AIPAC the basic requirement for peace: "Now is the time to lay aside once and for all the unrealistic vision of a Greater Israel. . . . Forswear annexation. Stop settlement activity. Reach out to the Palestinians as neighbors who deserve political rights."

These statements had a beneficial impact in the Middle East. For instance, when I visited Damascus in 1990, President Assad informed me that he was willing to negotiate with Israel on the status of the Golan Heights. His proposal was that both sides withdraw from the international border, with a small force of foreign observers and electronic devices to monitor the neutral zone. When I asked him if each nation would have to fall back an equal distance, he replied that Syria might move its troops farther from the border because of the terrain. He also gave me permission to report his proposal to Washington and to the Israelis, which I did in Jerusalem three days later. The following month I met with Yasir Arafat and other PLO leaders in Paris, where they all agreed to accept the Camp David Accords as a basis for future negotiations with the Israelis.

As usual, I reported these conversations to the White House and State Department, but at the time Washington did not seem to be interested.

There was no sustained American leadership in the Middle East peace process until after the Gulf War against Iraq in the spring of 1991, when Baker made several trips to the region. This resumption made possible a peace conference in Madrid in October 1991, convened jointly by the United States and the Soviet Union and attended by Israel, several Arab countries including Jordan, Lebanon, and Syria, and Palestinians from the occupied territories. Subsequently, more than a dozen formal rounds of bilateral talks were hosted by the United States, aimed at peace agreements between Israel and its immediate neighbors. The discussions between Israel and the Palestinians addressed a five-year interim agreement with hopes of negotiations on the permanent status issues. Although the Madrid effort brought no specific resolution of the issues, the willingness of the participants to communicate with one another reduced regional tensions and renewed hope of future progress toward peace.

Still, Israel put confiscation of Palestinian land ahead of peace, provoking an official White House statement: "The United States has opposed, and will continue to oppose, settlement activity in territories occupied in 1967, which remain an obstacle to peace." From the State Department, Secretary Baker added, "I don't think there is any greater obstacle to peace than settlement activity that continues not only unabated but at an advanced pace." As further proof of his seriousness, President George H. W. Bush demanded a freeze on settlement housing being built or planned, especially a large complex between Jerusalem and Bethlehem. When he finally threatened to withhold a portion of the $10 million daily aid package, plus loan guarantees, from the United States, the Israeli government complied and the U.S. grants and loans were approved—but with a deduction of $400 million, the amount that Israel already had spent on settlement activity. Later, after President Bush was no longer in office, I noticed that this major settlement was being rapidly completed.

Political leadership in Israel changed several times during this period, including formation of national unity governments that shifted authority back and forth between Labor and Likud leaders. After an election victory in June 1992, the Labor Party was able to form a coalition under the leadership of Prime Minister Yitzhak Rabin, without Likud participation. Israel then made clear its desire to reconcile differences with the Palestinians, Syria, and its other neighbors, and the Arab response was surprisingly positive.

# 9

## THE OSLO AGREEMENT

It was during this period of relative goodwill under Rabin's leadership that, without America's involvement, Norway's Foreign Minister Johann Holst, Professor Terje Larsen, and their wives helped to orchestrate highly secret peace talks between the government of Israel and the PLO. Israeli Foreign Minister Shimon Peres and Deputy Foreign Minister Yossi Beilin had a series of more than a dozen sessions, mostly in Oslo, with PLO leader Yasir Arafat's team, headed by Mahmoud Abbas (Abu Mazen) and Ahmed Qurei (Abu Ala). During the early months of 1993, both Peres and Arafat kept me informed about these efforts.

I was in the northern part of Yemen in August 1993 when I received an urgent request from Arafat to meet him in Saana. I returned to the capital city by helicopter and found the PLO leader almost beside himself with excitement. He told me that the peace talks had been successful and that the

Israelis were flying to the United States to inform the Clinton administration about the achievement. Above all else, Arafat emphasized the provision in the agreement that called for the formation of a Palestinian National Authority with the election of a president and members of a national assembly.

A few weeks later, Rosalynn and I were invited to a signing ceremony at the White House, where President Bill Clinton presided and Prime Minister Rabin and Chairman Arafat were to make a public declaration of peace. I was ushered to a prominent seat among the observers, along with other public officials, and my wife was a row or two behind me. I was surprised and embarrassed to see the Norwegians, Holst and Larsen, far back in the crowd and to notice that their key role in the peace effort was not mentioned.

In sum, the Oslo Agreement provided for a phased withdrawal of Israeli military forces from the West Bank, the establishment of a Palestinian governing authority with officials to be elected, and a five-year interim period during which the more difficult and specific issues would be negotiated. Although Rabin, Peres, and Arafat all received the Nobel Peace Prize for their historic achievement, there was strong opposition from radical elements on both sides.

As part of the agreement, in September 1993, Chairman Arafat sent a letter to Prime Minister Rabin in which he stated unequivocally that the PLO recognized the right of Israel to exist in peace and security, accepted U.N. Security

Council Resolutions 242 and 338, committed itself to a peaceful resolution of the conflict, renounced the use of terrorism and other acts of violence, affirmed that those articles of the PLO covenant that deny Israel's right to exist were no longer valid, and promised to submit these commitments to the Palestinian National Council for formal changes to the covenant.

Although Israel recognized the PLO as the sole representative of the Palestinians in the peace negotiations and promised five years of further progress, Arafat had failed to obtain other specific concessions concerning a timetable for Israel's withdrawal from occupied territories. In effect, what he got from the Oslo Agreement was the assurance of organizing a form of Palestinian government and staying in power so that he could administer Palestinian affairs in the West Bank and Gaza. The Israelis wanted and achieved much more.

It must be remembered that the status of Israelis in the West Bank and Gaza had changed dramatically in 1987 with the first intifada. Earlier, Israeli Jews in the West Bank had almost complete freedom of safe movement and required minimum military protection—about 10,000 troops in all the occupied territories. The relatively harmonious administration of local affairs by respected Palestinian notables already had been replaced in 1981 by Ariel Sharon with some "village leagues," often composed of outcast Palestinians who were willing to be hired by the Israelis. Dissension and danger prevailed. By 1988, no Israeli could travel in the area without Palestinian guides and some prior assurances of safe passage, and 180,000 Israeli troops were deployed to protect settlers and preserve the peace. With the Oslo Agreement, Israel's plan was that Arafat and the PLO would assume responsibility for local administration, free to receive and distribute (or perhaps retain a portion of) the international financial support that would be available to the Palestinians.

Following Oslo, Prime Minister Rabin emphasized that the agreement for which he had been honored had avoided the tight restrictions accepted by Menachem Begin at Camp David:

> We ourselves obtained this concession from the Palestinians—from those with whom one should make such deals—without any American promises as in the Camp David agreements. Jewish settlements will be placed under an exclusive Israeli jurisdiction; the [Palestinian] Autonomy Council will have no authority over them. The forces of the Israeli army will be redeployed in locations determined only by us, unlike the Camp David agreements which mandated a withdrawal of the Israeli army forces. In the agreement we reached we didn't consent to use the formula "withdrawal of Israeli army forces" except when it applied to the Gaza Strip. In application to all other places the only term used is "redeployment." . . . I

prefer that the Palestinians cope with the problem of enforcing order in Gaza. The Palestinians will be better at it than we were because they will allow no appeals to the Supreme Court and will prevent the [Israeli] Association for Civil Rights from criticizing the conditions there by denying it access to the area. They will rule there by their own methods, freeing— and this is most important—the Israeli army soldiers from having to do what they will do.

A key advantage that the Oslo Agreement gave to Israel was the shedding of formal responsibility for the living conditions and welfare of the territories' rapidly increasing population, still completely dominated by Israeli forces.

Prime Minister Rabin soon concluded a peace accord with Jordan and announced his willingness to negotiate with the Syrians, and he and Arafat concluded an agreement in May 1994 that applied to the Gaza Strip and to Jericho and its environs. It addressed four main issues: security arrangements, civil affairs, legal matters, and economic relations, and it pledged withdrawal of Israeli military forces from a number of Palestinian communities, including Gaza and Jericho, and a transfer of some civil authority from the Israeli Civil Administration to a Palestinian authority. There was also a commitment for elections to form a governmental structure for the Palestinians. The hope for further steps toward peace following the Oslo Agreement was severely damaged with the assassination of Rabin in November 1995 by an Israeli right-wing religious fanatic, who declared that his goal was to interrupt the peace process.

There was still some goodwill remaining from Oslo two months later, as indicated in this excerpt from President Clinton's memoir, *My Life*:

> Shimon Peres came to see me for the first time as prime minister, to reaffirm Israel's intention to turn over Gaza, Jericho, other major cities and 450 villages in the West Bank to the Palestinians by Christmas and to release at least another 1,000 Palestinian prisoners before the coming Israeli elections.

# 10

# THE PALESTINIAN ELECTION, 1996

One of the most important commitments of The Carter Center is to promote democracy in nations that face their first experience with elections or have a ruling party so powerful (or corrupt) that opposition candidates are hesitant to seek office. Although we have no authority over the local people, we respond to requests from governments, political parties, and national election officials to participate. Since our time and funding are limited, we offer our services only when we believe that our presence is necessary to ensure free and fair elections. Carter Center teams have monitored more than sixty elections, but three of the most interesting, challenging, and important have been for the Palestinian people.

Although I had met with other PLO leaders in Egypt and Syria beginning in 1983, my first personal meeting with Yasir Arafat was during a visit to Paris in April 1990. Rosalynn was with me to take notes, and Arafat had a large entourage of his top leaders. He was surprisingly friendly and obviously grateful to discuss Palestinian issues directly with a prominent American. His associates treated him with great deference, but Arafat was reluctant to give any clear answers to substantive and sensitive questions without first having a chance to reach a consensus among the many contending factions within his organization. He expressed his regrets at having rejected the Camp David Accords, admitting that he hadn't studied all its terms, including withdrawal of Israeli military and political forces from the occupied territories. He knew that I had called for a Palestinian homeland, pointed out that a democratic process would have to be the first step, and urged me to consider helping to ensure that Palestinians could elect their own government. I promised that, when the time came for any kind of election, The Carter Center and I would be deeply involved—provided we could obtain approval from Israel. I pushed him to fulfill his Oslo promise to modify the PLO charter to accept Israel's existence, but he was equivocal in his answer.

The Palestinian leader had never had any direct contact with Israeli leaders but was quite familiar with the different political factions that contended for leadership in Jerusalem. My notes show that he had specific questions about Prime Minister Shamir and some of the younger politicians, including Yossi Beilin (who later negotiated the Geneva Initiative) and Ehud Olmert (who would become prime minister). Although I had unofficial approval from Secretary of State

James Baker for what was supposed to be a private meeting, we decided to accept a last-minute invitation from President François Mitterrand to visit him at the Elysée Palace. This turned out to be a highly publicized event, which caused me some discomfort but was very gratifying to Arafat.

I maintained contact with Palestinian leaders after this introductory meeting, and when Israel approved an election for president and members of the Legislative Council as part of the Oslo Agreement, Arafat repeated his request to The Carter Center. We accepted the responsibility along with an organization with which we often cooperate, the National Democratic Institute (NDI), a nonprofit organization devoted to strengthening democracy. This was a very interesting experience, which illustrated many of the problems and challenges in the Holy Land. When we arrived there in January 1996, it was obvious that the Israelis had almost complete control over every aspect of political, military, and economic existence of the Palestinians within the West Bank and Gaza. Israeli settlements permeated the occupied territories, and highways connecting the settlements with one another and with Jerusalem were being rapidly built, with Palestinians prohibited from using or crossing some of the key roads. In addition, more than one hundred permanent Israeli checkpoints obstructed the routes still open to Palestinian traffic, either pedestrian or vehicular.

After meeting with other members of our observer team, I had sessions with American diplomats, Palestinian pollsters, political candidates, and members of the Election Commission. I learned that the commission had been in existence for only four weeks and that political candidates had just three weeks to campaign, but seven hundred had qualified for the eighty-eight parliamentary seats, six of which were set aside for Christians and one for a Samaritan. Only Arafat and a relatively unknown woman named Samiha Khalil had qualified for the presidency.

There were many problems, which I discussed with Prime Minister Shimon Peres and General Uri Dayan, who was responsible for security in the West Bank and Gaza. They assured me that key checkpoints would be opened, Israeli soldiers would not enter voting places, and voters would not be intimidated. I had seen many posters in East Jerusalem that threatened any Arab voters with the loss of their identification cards, housing permits, and social services. Israeli leaders, who told me that a militant religious group had posted the warnings, promised to remove as many of them as possible. The biggest problem related to East Jerusalem, which Palestinians (and the international community) consider to be their occupied territory and Israelis claim as an integral part of their nation.

The key question concerning the election was whether Palestinians living in East Jerusalem were voting as residents or as aliens who were casting absentee ballots to be counted outside the disputed area. There were about 200,000 resident Arabs, only about 4,000 of whom would be given permits to vote—and then only in five post offices, four of them quite small. Of about 120,000 registered voters, the others who had adequate determination and transportation might find their way outside Jerusalem to nearby polling sites in suburban villages, including the Mount of Olives, Ramallah, Bethany, and Bethlehem. This was a very sensitive political issue, and a failure to resolve it threatened the conduct of the election.

Rosalynn and I met with Yasir Arafat in Gaza City, where he was staying with his wife, Suha, and their little daughter. The baby, dressed in a beautiful pink suit, came readily to sit on my lap, where I practiced the same wiles that had been successful with our children and grandchildren. A lot of photographs were taken, and then the photographers asked that Arafat hold his daughter for a while. When he took her, the child screamed loudly and reached out her hands to me, bringing jovial admonitions to the presidential candidate to stay at home enough to become acquainted with his own child. During our more serious time together, I chastised Arafat for arresting Palestinian members of the news media and human rights activists, but he was unrepentant, claiming that they had stirred up strife between Muslims and Christians. I urged him to modify the Palestine National Charter to renounce violence and to recognize Israel, but he claimed that this had already been accomplished during the Oslo peace process. I also urged him to give the newly elected Legislative Council maximum autonomy, and he promised to do so, stating that they would assemble for the first time shortly after Ramadan (an annual month of fasting and prayer for Muslims that would begin that same weekend).

At Arafat's request, I then met with Mahmoud al-Zahar and other leaders of Hamas, an Islamic militant group that opposed recognition of Israel, perpetrated acts of violence, and was increasingly competitive with Arafat's secular Fatah Party. I urged them to accept the results of the election and forgo violence. They promised not to disrupt the elections and to renounce violence in the future "if Israelis discontinue repression." They informed me that they intended to participate in later municipal elections but not to be part of the Legislative Council.

The issue of voting in East Jerusalem became critical before voting was to begin, and we finally worked out a compromise: to have the slots in the top edges of the ballot boxes! Palestinians could claim they were dropping in their ballots vertically as on-site votes while Israelis could maintain that the envelopes were being inserted horizontally as letters to be mailed.

On election day Rosalynn and I went from one polling station to another, and our observers heard complaints and resolved as many as we could. Quite early there were few voters in East Jerusalem, and about fifty uniformed Israeli police were around the entrances and even within the post offices, ostentatiously videotaping the face of every Palestinian who was standing in line to cast a ballot. Two domestic observers who appeared at the largest post office with their proper credentials were arrested, and one was beaten on the way to jail.

This news spread like wildfire throughout Jerusalem. At the main checkpoint where the Palestinians were going outside the city to vote, a young captain told me that his orders were to record every name. I called General Dayan to report these problems, and the checkpoints were opened, but it was around noon before the police numbers at the Jerusalem sites were reduced and the final video cameras put away. Dayan's reasoning was that they were restraining right-wing Israelis to prevent violence, but it was obvious that the Palestinian voters were intimidated, and only about 1,600 Jerusalem voters finally cast (or mailed) ballots in the city.

During the day our observer team collected and analyzed reports from about 250 voting places. Overall, about 75 percent of all registered voters cast their ballots, and in Gaza more than 85 percent voted. Of 1,696 voting places outside Jerusalem, there were problems in only two. Three Palestinians were shot and killed by Israeli police at a checkpoint at Jenin, but 60 percent of the people voted in the village. The participation and enthusiasm of women was the biggest surprise for us. In Gaza and most other places where few women were ever seen in public, they jammed the polling sites.

Yasir Arafat received 88 percent of votes for president and members of his Fatah Party and affiliated independents won about 75 percent of the Legislative Council seats. After the election, I again urged that he honor the independence of the elected council, make a credible offer to Hamas and others to participate in the future, set an early date for municipal elections, and expedite the amendments to the PLO charter. Some strong independents were elected, including Hanan Ashrawi, an influential Christian spokesperson from Ramallah. Everyone laughed when Arafat told me there were going to be about fifteen women on the council, adding that "Hanan counts for ten."

It was obvious that release of almost 5,000 of the Palestinian prisoners being held by the Israelis and the possibility of progress on the permanent issues would be predicated on good-faith action by both sides. Prime Minister Peres announced that all members of the Palestinian National Council (legislative body of the PLO) would be permitted to travel to the West Bank and Gaza in order to amend the PLO charter. This was welcome news, since many of the more active members of the Fatah Party had long been accused by the Israelis of being terrorists and not given travel permits within their own land. The new president established his office in Ramallah and continued the struggle to obtain complete Palestinian control of the West Bank and Gaza, which remained occupied by Israel.

All of us international observers were pleased with the quality of the election, which was nothing less than an overwhelming mandate, not only for forming a Palestinian government but also for reconciliation between Israelis and Palestinians. We also were reminded of the extreme sensitivity and difficulty of issues still to be resolved.

# 11

## BILL CLINTON'S
## PEACE EFFORTS

Unfortunately for the peace process, Palestinian terrorists carried out two lethal suicide bombings in March 1996, a few weeks after the Palestinian election. Thirty-two Israeli citizens were killed, an act that probably gave the Likud's hawkish candidate, Binyamin Netanyahu, a victory over Prime Minister Shimon Peres. The new leader of Israel promised never to exchange land for peace. Foreign Minister Ariel Sharon declared the Oslo Agreement to be "national suicide" and stated, "Everybody has to move, run and grab as many hilltops as they can to enlarge the settlements because everything we take now will stay ours. . . . Everything we don't grab will go to them." This policy precipitated Israel's tightened hold on the occupied territories and aroused further violence from the Palestinians.

With Arafat now an officially elected leader, President Bill Clinton made strong and sustained efforts to find some

**Map 6**

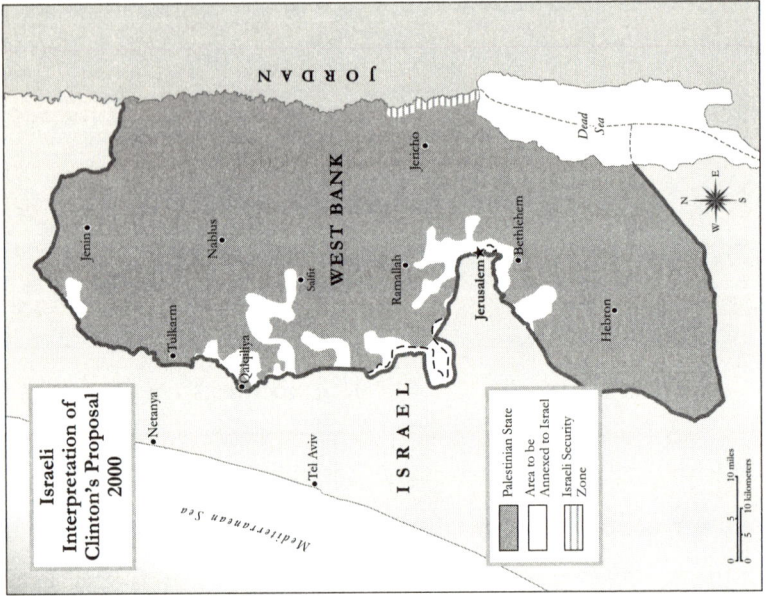

Israeli Interpretation of Clinton's Proposal 2000

WEST BANK

JORDAN

ISRAEL

*Mediterranean Sea*

*Dead Sea*

Jenin
Nablus
Tulkarm
Qalqilya
Salfit
Ramallah
Jericho
Jerusalem
Bethlehem
Hebron
Netanya
Tel Aviv

Palestinian State
Area to be Annexed to Israel
Israeli Security Zone

0   5   10 miles
0   5   10 kilometers

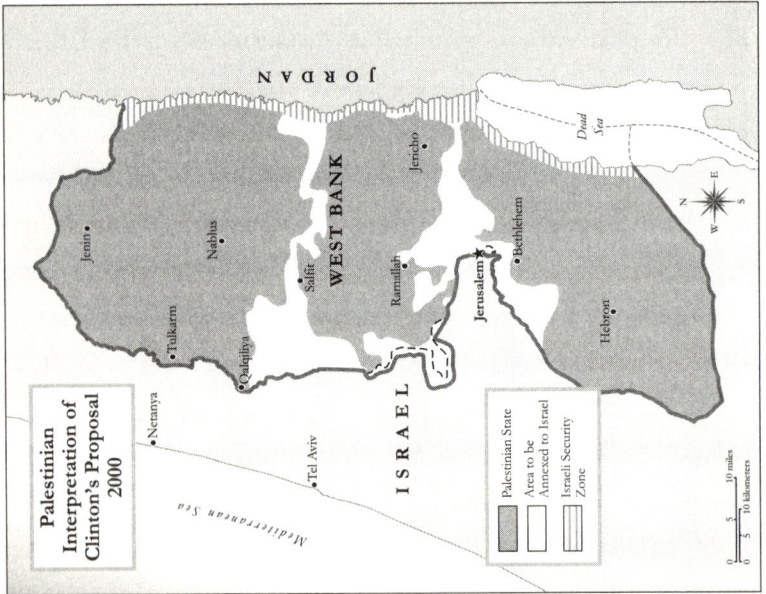

Palestinian Interpretation of Clinton's Proposal 2000

WEST BANK

JORDAN

ISRAEL

*Mediterranean Sea*

*Dead Sea*

Jenin
Nablus
Tulkarm
Qalqilya
Salfit
Ramallah
Jericho
Jerusalem
Bethlehem
Hebron
Netanya
Tel Aviv

Palestinian State
Area to be Annexed to Israel
Israeli Security Zone

0   5   10 miles
0   5   10 kilometers

reasonable accommodation between Israelis and Palestinians. A nine-day summit conference was convened at Wye Plantation in Maryland in October 1998, during which some agreements were reached involving redeployment of Israeli troops, security arrangements, prisoner releases, and the resumption of permanent status negotiations, but within a few weeks the Israeli cabinet voted to postpone execution of the Wye River Memorandum.

Even after the Labor Party's Ehud Barak was elected as prime minister in May 1999, there was a sustained commitment by Israel's government to avoid full compliance with the Oslo Agreement or with key U.N. Resolutions 242 and 338, while Palestinians were reluctant to abandon any of them as the basis for permanent peace. Despite these handicaps, the United States sponsored a series of peace talks at Sharm al-Sheikh, at Bolling Air Force Base, and then at Camp David for a fourteen-day session in July 2000.

In September 2000, with Prime Minister Barak's reluctant approval, Ariel Sharon and an escort of several hundred policemen went to the Temple Mount complex, site of the Dome of the Rock and al-Aqsa Mosque, where he declared that the Islamic holy site would remain under permanent Israeli control. The former military leader was accused by many Israelis of purposely inflaming emotions to provoke a furious response and obstruct any potential success of ongoing peace talks. Combining their reaction to this event with their frustration over Israel's failure to implement the Oslo Agreement, the Palestinians responded with a further outbreak of violence, which was to be known as the second intifada.

Later, during his last months in Washington, President Clinton made what he called his final proposal. Eighty percent of Israeli settlers would remain in the West Bank, and Israel could maintain its control of the Jordan River valley and an early-warning capability within the West Bank, with an additional provision for emergency deployments to meet security needs. The new state of Palestine would be demilitarized, with an international force for border security and deterrence and Palestinian sovereignty over their airspace—except for special arrangements to meet Israeli training and operational needs.

In Jerusalem, the Arab neighborhoods would be administered by Palestinians and the Jewish neighborhoods by Israel, with Palestinian sovereignty over the Temple Mount and Israeli sovereignty over the Western Wall and the "holy place" of which it is a part. Palestinian refugees could return only to the West Bank and Gaza. It was stipulated that, if accepted, this agreement would replace *all* the requirements of U.N. resolutions that applied to the Middle East. There was no clear response from Prime Minister Barak, but he later stated that Israel had twenty pages of reservations. President Arafat also rejected the proposal.

As President Clinton made efforts to promote peace, there was a 90 percent growth in the number of settlers in the occupied territories, with the greatest increase during the administration of Prime Minister Ehud Barak. By the end of the year 2000, Israeli settlers in the West Bank and Gaza numbered 225,000. The best offer to the Palestinians—by Clinton, not Barak—had been to withdraw 20 percent of the settlers, leaving more than 180,000 in 209 settlements, covering about 10 percent of the occupied land, including land to be "leased" and portions of the Jordan River valley and East Jerusalem.

The percentage figure is misleading, since it usually includes only the actual footprints of the settlements. There is a zone with a radius of about four hundred meters around each settlement within which Palestinians cannot enter. In addition, there are other large areas that would have been taken or earmarked to be used exclusively by Israel, roadways that connect the settlements to one another and to Jerusalem, and "life arteries" that provide the settlers with water, sewage, electricity, and communications. These range in width from five hundred to four thousand meters, and Palestinians cannot use or cross many of these connecting links. This honeycomb of settlements and their interconnecting conduits effectively divide the West Bank into at least two noncontiguous areas and multiple fragments, often uninhabitable or even unreachable, and control of the Jordan River valley denies Palestinians any direct access eastward into Jordan. About one hundred military checkpoints completely surround Palestine and block routes going into or between Palestinian communities, combined with an uncountable number of other roads that are permanently closed with large concrete cubes or mounds of earth and rocks.

There was no possibility that any Palestinian leader could accept such terms and survive, but official statements from Washington and Jerusalem were successful in placing the entire onus for the failure on Yasir Arafat. Violence in the Holy Land continued.

There were still some remaining pro forma commitments to the Oslo Agreement's "final status" peace talks to deal with Jerusalem, refugees, settlements, security arrangements, borders, and relations and cooperation with neighboring countries. A new round of talks was held at Taba in January 2001, just as George W. Bush became president, between President Arafat and the Israeli foreign minister, and it was later claimed that the Palestinians rejected a "generous offer" put forward by Prime Minister Barak with Israel keeping only 5 percent of the West Bank. The fact is that no such offers were ever made. Barak later said, "It was plain to me that there was no chance of reaching a settlement at Taba. Therefore I said there would be no negotiations and there would be no delegation and there would be no official discussions and no documentation. Nor would Americans be present in the room. The only thing that took place at Taba were non-binding contacts between senior Israelis and senior Palestinians."*

---

*Despite this official disclaimer, substantive discussions were held at Taba, which proved to be the foundation for what evolved into the Geneva Initiative, to be described in Chapter 13.

**Map 7**

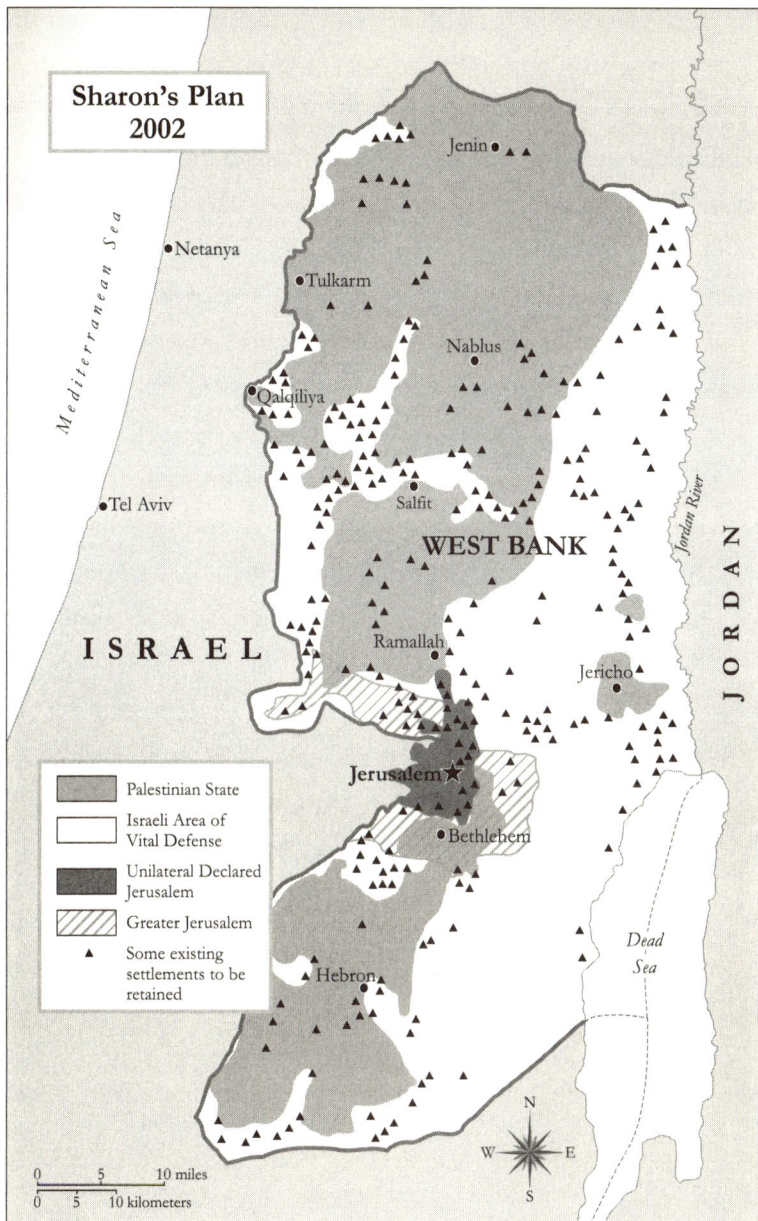

Sharon's Plan
2002

Mediterranean Sea

•Netanya

•Tulkarm

Jenin• ▲ ▲

Nablus
•

•Qalqiliya

•Tel Aviv

Salfit

**WEST BANK**

**ISRAEL**

Ramallah
•

Jericho
•

*Jordan River*

**J O R D A N**

Jerusalem★

•Bethlehem

Dead
Sea

Palestinian State

Israeli Area of
Vital Defense

Unilateral Declared
Jerusalem

Greater Jerusalem

▲  Some existing
settlements to be
retained

Hebron▲

0     5     10 miles
0     5     10 kilometers

N
W     E
S

*153*

The election of Ariel Sharon as prime minister two months later brought an end to these efforts to find accommodation.

A government statement affirmed Israel's aspiration to achieve peace but declared that all negotiating failures had been due to the ongoing and escalating Palestinian terrorism supported by the Palestinian Authority. As the chief spokesperson for the Palestinians, responsible for promoting peace and human rights, Dr. Hanan Ashrawi responded to Israel's claims:

> So far, they have succeeded in holding the peace process hostage to this mentality on the one hand. And on the other hand they have provoked tremendous violence by acts of incitement like shelling, bombing, house demolition, uprooting trees, destroying crops, assassinating political leaders, placing all Palestinians under closure in a state of total immobility—a prison. And then they wonder why some Palestinians are acting violently! And then they want to have the right to exercise violence against the captive population. Then they like to make non-violence on the part of the Palestinians a precondition for the Palestinians to qualify for talks, let alone for statehood.

# 12

## THE
## GEORGE W. BUSH
## YEARS

A national election in Israel occurred soon after the inauguration of George W. Bush in January 2001. Well known for having been aggressive in dealing with Palestinians, Ariel Sharon was easily elected prime minister within the troubled environment of the new intifada. He strongly opposed the Oslo peace agreement and emphasized his total commitment to counteract attacks on Israeli citizens and armed forces—almost all of which were occurring on Palestinian territory.

Violence increased during this second intifada, costing the lives of more than a thousand Palestinians and nearly two hundred Israelis, and late in March three crucial events occurred, almost simultaneously. On March 27, a suicide bomber took his own life in an explosion that killed thirty Israelis in the midst of a Passover holiday celebration at the Park Hotel in Netanya, a coastal city. Instant condemnations of terrorist acts came from leaders around the world, including American officials and the U.N. Secretary-General.

The next day, at the Arab League meeting in Beirut, twenty-two nations ended a long debate by endorsing a resolution introduced by Saudi Crown Prince (soon to be King) Abdullah. It offered Israel normal relations with all Arab states if Israel complied with U.N. Resolutions 194 and 242. Asked how "normal relations" were defined, the Saudis responded, "We envision a relationship between the Arab countries and Israel that is exactly like the relationship between the Arab countries and any other state." They further explained that "all occupied Arab territories" and "the return of refugees" were deliberately vague enough to allow the Israelis to settle those matters through negotiations with the Palestinians, Syrians, and Lebanese.

The White House responded: "President George W. Bush urges other leaders to build on the Crown Prince's ideas to address the cause of peace in the troubled region."

The next day, March 29, a massive Israeli military force surrounded and destroyed Yasir Arafat's office compound in Ramallah, leaving only a few rooms intact. Claiming that Arafat was supporting the intifada, Prime Minister Sharon informed members of his cabinet that he wanted to arrest Arafat and expel him from the Palestinian territories. "The only commitment we've made," Police Minister Uzi Landau announced, "is not to kill him." Secretary of State Colin Powell called for Sharon to "consider the consequences" of his actions and limit civilian casualties, and later the United States voted for a U.N. Security Council resolution demanding Israeli withdrawal from Ramallah, which Israel had declared to be under Palestinian self-rule in 1995. Israel ignored the resolution.

Arab diplomats accused Sharon of deliberately sabotaging the Arab peace overture, and Crown Prince Abdullah called the prime minister's assault on Arafat "a brutal, despicable, savage, inhumane and cruel action." Except for one brief interlude, Arafat was to be permanently confined to this small space until the final days of his life. Having limited contacts with his own people and with minimal remaining authority, he was still held responsible by the Israelis for every act of violence within the occupied territories.

Responding to strong international pressure to break the costly impasse, in June 2002, President George W. Bush announced a two-state solution for the Israeli-Palestinian conflict, which was the first time an American leader had described the future Palestinian government as potentially sovereign. However, the president precluded any further involvement in the process by the Palestinians' only elected leader, Yasir Arafat, declaring, "Peace requires a new and different Palestinian leadership, so that a Palestinian state can be born." Responsibility for a lack of progress toward peace was placed on the Palestinians, and President Bush and

Prime Minister Sharon declared that the response to any violent actions on their part was to be equated with the global war against terrorism.

The only American demands on the Israelis were that they return to the military positions they had occupied before September 2000, when violence had erupted after Sharon's visit to the Temple Mount, refrain from any new settlement activity in the occupied territories, and negotiate terms sometime in the future for ultimate compliance with U.N. Resolution 242, after the Palestinians demonstrated their ability to stop all violent resistance in the occupied territories. Prime Minister Sharon quickly accepted the elements of the proposal that concerned Palestinian violence. The Palestinians maintained that almost 200,000 Israeli occupying troops could not prevent *every* act of potential violence, and it would not be possible for their imprisoned and isolated leader to guarantee total peace, especially with only a few of their security force permitted to have sidearms or communications equipment.

Since Arafat was not acceptable to Bush or Sharon as an interlocutor, Mahmoud Abbas (Abu Mazen) was chosen as the first prime minister of the Palestinian Authority in March 2003. Abbas was known as "the face of Palestinian moderation" and the chief architect of the Oslo Agreement; his choice was strongly supported by Israel and the United States. Arafat also responded favorably, claiming that this change was just an endorsement of his own reform efforts. In fact, it led to no genuine peace talks with Israel and to a struggle between Abbas and Arafat over control of security services.

In April 2003 a "Roadmap" for resolving the Israeli-Palestinian conflict was announced by U.N. Secretary-General Kofi Annan on behalf of the United States, the United Nations, Russia, and the European Union (known as the Quartet). Annan stated,

> Such a settlement, negotiated between the parties, will result in the emergence of an independent, democratic Palestinian state living side by side in peace and security with Israel and its other neighbors. The settlement will end the occupation that began in 1967, based on the Madrid Conference terms of reference and the principle of land for peace, U.N. Security Council Resolutions 242, 338 and 1397, agreements previously reached by the parties, and the Arab initiative proposed by Saudi Crown Prince Abdullah and endorsed by the Arab Summit in Beirut.

The Palestinians accepted the road map in its entirety, but the Israeli government announced fourteen caveats and prerequisites, some of which would preclude any final peace talks (see Appendix 7 for the full list). Israeli provisos included:

1. The total dismantling of *all* militant Palestinian sub-groups, collection of *all* illegal weapons, and their destruction;

2. Cessation of incitement against Israel, but the Roadmap cannot state that Israel must cease violence and incitement against the Palestinians;

3. Israeli control over Palestine, including the entry and exit of all persons and cargo, plus its airspace and electromagnetic spectrum (radio, television, radar, etc.);

4. The waiver of any right of return of refugees to Israel;

5. No discussion of Israeli settlement in Judaea, Samaria, and Gaza or the status of the Palestinian Authority and its institutions in Jerusalem;

6. No reference to the key provisions of U.N. Resolution 242.

The practical result of all this is that the Roadmap for Peace has become moot, with only two results: Israel has been able to use it as a delaying tactic with an endless series of preconditions that can never be met, while proceeding with plans to implement its unilateral goals; and the United States has been able to give the impression of positive engagement in a "peace process," which President Bush has announced will not be fulfilled during his time in office.

A Middle East summit meeting, hosted by Jordanian King Abdullah II and attended by President Bush, Prime Minister Sharon, and Prime Minister Abbas, was held in Aqaba, Jordan, in June 2003 for a general discussion of the Roadmap's step-by-step process. Some phrases of the closing statements were quite interesting, as I have italicized. Israeli Prime Minister Ariel Sharon said,

> The Government and people of Israel welcome the opportunity to renew direct negotiations according to the steps of the Roadmap *as adopted by the Israeli government.* . . . We can also reassure our Palestinian partners that we understand the importance of territorial contiguity in the West Bank, for a viable, Palestinian state. Israeli policy in the territories *that are subject to direct negotiations* with the Palestinians will reflect this fact. . . .
>
> We accept the principle that *no unilateral actions* by any party can prejudge the outcome of our negotiations.

President George Bush responded, "I'm also pleased to be with Prime Minister Abbas. He represents the cause of freedom and statehood for the Palestinian people. I strongly support that cause. . . . In addition, Prime Minister Sharon has stated that *no unilateral actions* by either side can or should prejudge the outcome of future negotiations."

Abbas resigned from his post in October, citing his exclusion from substantive peace efforts by Israel and the United States and some opposition to his role from within the PLO.

Although the initial proposals and timetable for the Roadmap for Peace have been largely ignored or abandoned, the statement on basic elements of a permanent two-state solution to the Israeli-Palestinian conflict have been retained by the Quartet members, including an end of the occupation begun in 1967 and full commitment to the key U.N. resolutions.

The International Quartet realizes that Israel must have a lasting and comprehensive peace. This will not be possible unless Israel accepts the terms of the Roadmap and reverses its colonizing the internationally recognized Palestinian territory, and unless the Palestinians respond by accepting Israel's right to exist, free of violence.

# 13

## THE GENEVA INITIATIVE

With concerted peace talks going nowhere after Ariel Sharon and George W. Bush took office, a group of Israelis and Palestinians continued to build upon the Taba talks. Leaders of the effort were former Israeli deputy prime minister Beilin and former Palestinian minister of information and culture Yasser Abed Rabbo. In October 2001, I had a call from Beilin, an experienced political leader who had been in the forefront of peace efforts, including the Oslo negotiations and those of more recent years. He had consulted with his associates in Egypt and the PLO, who suggested that I might be of help in resolving some differences that had arisen in the negotiations between Israelis and Palestinians.

I met with Beilin that same month, and he described their ongoing efforts to reach an agreement on the three most difficult issues: settlements, including permanent boundaries;

the right of return of Palestinians; and Jerusalem. The ultimate goal would be to issue a peace proposal, evolved without official Israeli or Palestinian government endorsement, which would be fair, balanced, and potentially acceptable to both sides. In such an unofficial arrangement, I did not feel constrained to get the usual approval from Washington for my participation.

Beilin and I communicated regularly, and about a year later he felt that there would soon be something to report to the world. We believed that a majority of Israelis and Palestinians would welcome a comprehensive agreement even if it meant making substantial concessions on settlements and the other major issues. The extensive talks had produced key points of accommodation, including a potential boundary based on detailed aerial photographs that would expand the internationally recognized area of Israel into the West Bank enough to encompass about half of the Israeli settlers living there. Reasonable proposals regarding shared access to Jerusalem and the limited right of return of Palestinians were also included.

Although there was still much work to be done, I promised to help with publicity and promotion once a final agreement was reached. In October 2002 I learned that I had been awarded the Nobel Peace Prize, and I proposed that the forthcoming awards ceremonies in Oslo and Stockholm would provide an opportunity to unveil the peace proposal and attract world attention to it. However, the Swedish gov-

**Map 8**

Geneva
Initiative
2003

Nazareth•

Jenin•

Netanya•

*Mediterranean Sea*

Nablus•

**WEST BANK**

Tel Aviv•

*Jordan River*

**JORDAN**

N
W   E
S

Ramallah•

Jerusalem★

**ISRAEL**

•Hebron

*Dead Sea*

Gaza•

**GAZA
STRIP**

Rafah•

•Beersheba

**EGYPT**

*NEGEV*

Green Line

Annexed to Israel

Annexed to
Palestinian Areas

| 0 | 10 | 20 miles |
| 0 | 10 | 20 kilometers |

ernment rejected this request from Beilin and Rabbo because of its potentially controversial nature, and to avoid confusion with Nobel events. With more discussions needed, I sent the director of The Carter Center conflict resolution program to work with the negotiators.

The final draft was concluded in October 2003, and I published an op-ed article describing the peace proposal and then delivered the keynote address in Geneva, Switzerland, in December to a large audience of Israelis, Palestinians, and influential world leaders at a launching ceremony and celebration.

The Initiative provides for secure borders and overwhelming recognition by the Arab world for Israel and a sovereign, contiguous, viable state for Palestinians recognized by the international community. More specifically, the dividing border would be based on the 1967 lines but with a mutual exchange of land, giving Israel some of its largest settlements, Jewish neighborhoods in East Jerusalem, and the Jewish Quarter of the Old City. An international religious authority would control central holy sites, with the Temple Mount officially under Palestinian sovereignty and the Western Wall and Jewish Quarter of the Old City under Israeli sovereignty. Israel would decide unilaterally how many Palestinian refugees would be admitted to Israel, and other refugees could return to Palestine or receive appropriate compensation as a fulfillment of U.N. General Assembly Resolution 194.*

*The complete text of the Geneva Initiative can be found at www. peacenow.org.

Although it is an unofficial document that will require modifications if and when official and sincere peace talks are held, the Geneva Initiative envisions a reasonable and mutually acceptable permanent agreement. An overwhelming number of both Israelis and Palestinians want a durable two-state solution, based on well-known criteria that have been spelled out in the Quartet's Roadmap and are compatible with the Geneva Initiative. Polling by the James Baker Institute revealed that a majority of Israelis and Palestinians approved the Geneva principles, despite strong opposition from some top political leaders.

There were public endorsements from Prime Minister Tony Blair, President Jacques Chirac, President Bill Clinton, and about eighty other world leaders and Nobel laureates including Nelson Mandela, Lech Walesa, and John Hume. The most significant fact is that the Geneva Initiative overcomes what seems to be a fatal (perhaps deliberate) flaw of the Roadmap: the easily delayed or aborted step-by-step procedure that could postpone decisive negotiations indefinitely. Sharon condemned the Geneva Initiative and there was silence from the White House, but Secretary of State Colin Powell supported the Initiative and met with the key negotiators for a personal briefing. Arafat approved the process but did not endorse the final text, and the more militant Palestinian factions condemned the proposal's abandonment of the full right of return of displaced Arabs to Israel and the West Bank.

The Geneva proposals made a substantial impact in Israel and may have brought about a dramatic change in policy. Contravening the rejection of unilateral action made by Prime Minister Sharon at Aqaba a year earlier, in June 2004 Israel's cabinet approved a plan for disengagement from the Gaza Strip without consultation with the Palestinian leaders. This proposal was welcomed by the United States and approved by most Palestinians. Living among 1.3 million Palestinians, the 8,000 Israeli settlers were controlling 40 percent of the arable land and more than one-half the water resources, and 12,000 troops were required to defend their presence.

# 14

## THE PALESTINIAN ELECTION, 2005

Yasir Arafat died in November 2004, and Palestinian law required that his successor be elected within a few weeks. Once again, The Carter Center was asked to observe the process, with the National Democratic Institute as a partner.

I arrived in Israel on January 6, 2005, and my first meeting was with Prime Minister Sharon, who immediately expressed confidence that he had sufficient votes in the Knesset to overcome opposition to the Gaza withdrawal. He estimated that about 30 percent of the settlers would leave voluntarily (with generous monetary compensation) and the others would resist, perhaps a small number even with violence. The southern Negev, the location of his own family farm, was to be their primary destination for resettlement. We exchanged reminiscences of our joint experiences during the past years, and I thanked him for his positive influence on Prime Minister Begin when I was negotiating peace agreements as president. He stated that Israeli checkpoints would be manned by soldiers during the Palestinian election but would not impede traffic, and that military forces would be withdrawn from the major cities. Having observed Sharon in action for almost three decades, I had no doubt that he would fulfill his promises.

Although our team maintained complete neutrality among competing candidates, our hope was that the election of a moderate and respected leader would bring an early resumption of the long-stalled peace process. I urged Sharon to be more flexible in permitting Palestinians to vote in East Jerusalem, but his response was that the arrangements of 1996 would prevail. He reminded me that I had been instrumental in negotiating the agreements and added that no Palestinian polling officials or domestic observers would be allowed to enter the post offices, which would be manned by Israeli employees. Any "disruptive" campaigning would also be forbidden. In fact, one presidential candidate was arrested the next day when he attempted to seek votes among a small crowd near the Lion's Gate.

It was obvious to all international observers who spread throughout the occupied territories that the Palestinian people had little freedom of movement or independent activity—a situation unlikely to change as long as they were surrounded by troops and walls and their land was occupied by Israeli settlers. Prior to election day, we observers had our customary meetings with leading candidates and members of the Central Election Commission. They were confident about their own preparations but concerned that possible violence might erupt because of interference by Israeli officials in preventing Arab voting in East Jerusalem.

Whenever I visit a foreign country, I look for opportunities to leave the capital city and visit interesting places. While our observer teams were moving to their posts on Saturday morning, the other delegation leaders joined me in a visit to Nazareth Village, a site that has been developed to emulate the community of Jesus during his youth. Beginning in 1996, Rosalynn and I have joined other Christians, mostly Mennonites, in acquiring land and raising funds for its development. The ten-acre site is in the heart of the city, and we were impressed by its high quality and archaeological and historical integrity.

As is our practice, we moved constantly throughout election day, visiting twenty-two voting sites, beginning with the post offices within East Jerusalem, where problems always arise. It quickly became apparent that the Israeli officials had voters' lists that were completely different from the names of people who came to cast ballots, and by noon there had been practically no voting—just a growing crowd of angry Palestinians. At the main polling site, the only post office larger than a mobile home, there were 3,500 names on the list, with one Israeli clerk checking credentials of potential voters and methodically turning them away. When I finally threatened to call an international press conference, the prime minister's office agreed to ignore the lists and permit all persons registered in Jerusalem to vote at any site, but only international observers and no Palestinians could monitor this process. By this time it was two p.m., and we were able to salvage the participation of only a small number of voters. I also visited Bethlehem and other places in the West Bank and found few problems there or in Gaza.

I was up early the next morning to assess the reports of our observer team and to prepare a political analysis and private letter of advice for delivery to Mahmoud Abbas, who had been elected overwhelmingly. I finished these tasks in time to meet before daybreak with leading birding experts from Israel and Palestine, Yossi Leshem and Imad Atrash. We first went to a fifty-acre park in the heart of Jerusalem's urban area, where we watched twenty-four gazelles that live there with no fences or walls to separate them from the adjacent buildings and heavily traveled roadways. We then drove to a small park in the shadow of the Knesset building to observe the netting, banding, and release of migratory birds that fly over the Holy Land to circumvent the Mediterranean Sea. It was wonderful to see Jewish and Arab ornithologists working in harmony on these projects.

After joining our delegation leaders to conclude generally positive statements about the election, I went to Ramallah to meet with Abbas and his key advisers. The Israelis had ruled out any negotiation with Arafat, and now they would

have the partner they had seemed to want. I outlined my
thoughts and gave Abbas my written notes, presuming that
the new president would soon be engaged in direct talks with
Israeli leaders. He reported that the inauguration ceremony
would be in two days but expressed doubts that the Israelis
wanted peace talks. The Palestinian group's opinion was that
both Sharon and Deputy Prime Minister Ehud Olmert had
long wanted to abandon Gaza while concentrating on the
colonization of the West Bank. They pointed out that Palestinian leaders had accepted all provisions of the Quartet's
Roadmap for Peace, but that Sharon had publicly rejected
most of its key provisions.

There was no doubt that Abbas had the support and respect of his people and that he was dedicated to the immediate pursuit of a peace agreement in accordance with the
Roadmap. He needed the full support of American and Israeli leaders as he struggled to forge at least a partially
trained and equipped security force, deal with a crumbling
economy, and earn the respect and support of the international community. Also, the members of his Fatah Party
faced the imminent political challenge of Hamas Party representatives, who were showing impressive success in local
elections and had announced their intention to field a full
slate of candidates in the upcoming campaign for the Legislative Council. This would be a contest between the long-
dominant political organization of Arafat and the PLO and a
much more militant group that refused to acknowledge Is-

rael's right to exist and insisted on the right to use violence against Israelis, whom they considered to be enemies occupying their land.

It was on this trip that we saw the most disturbing intrusions of the great dividing wall being built by the Israelis, which I will assess in Chapter 16. Described as a "security fence" whose declared function was to deter Palestinian attacks against Israelis, its other purpose became clear as we observed its construction and examined maps of the barrier's ultimate path through Palestine. Including the Israeli-occupied Jordan River valley, the wall would take in large areas of land for Israel and encircle the Palestinians who remained in their remnant of the West Bank. This would severely restrict Palestinian access to the outside world. "Imprisonment wall" is more descriptive than "security fence."

After returning to America, I went to the White House and gave a personal report to President Bush, emphasizing my concern about Israel's rejection of the Roadmap's terms and the building of the wall. I also relayed Mahmoud Abbas's desire to begin comprehensive peace talks at an early date. The president repeated his commitment to the Roadmap and said that his new secretary of state, Condoleezza Rice, was taking office that same day and that one of her top priorities would be a persistent and aggressive search for peace between Israel and the Palestinians.

The Israeli settlers were removed from Gaza in August 2005, with 50,000 troops there to minimize violence. This left behind the Arab inhabitants of the tiny area. There was some predictable controversy in Israel, with extreme right-wingers bitterly opposed to any withdrawals of Israeli settlers and with some peace groups claiming that unilateral actions would lead to the abandonment of long-range peace proposals.

Let's take a quick look at Gaza. Its population has soared in recent years as Palestinian refugees have poured in from other areas occupied by Israel. In 1948 there were 90,000 natives, the population more than tripled by 1967, and there are now more than 1.4 million—3,700 people living within each square kilometer. Although there are metropolitan areas with greater population density (such as Manhattan), this is supposed to be a self-sufficient entity, similar to a small and isolated state—separated from the West Bank by forty kilometers of Israeli territory.

Gaza has maintained a population growth rate of 4.7 percent annually, one of the highest in the world, so more than half its people are less than fifteen years old. They are being strangled since the Israeli "withdrawal," surrounded by a separation barrier that is penetrated only by Israeli-controlled checkpoints, with just a single opening (for personnel only) into Egypt's Sinai as their access to the outside world. There have been no moves by Israel to permit transportation by sea or by air. Fishermen are not permitted to leave the harbor, workers are prevented from going to outside jobs, the import or export of food and other goods is severely restricted and often cut off completely, and the police, teachers, nurses, and social workers are deprived of salaries. Per capita income has decreased 40 percent during the last three years, and the poverty rate has reached 70 percent. The U.N. Special Rapporteur on the Right to Food has stated that acute malnutrition in Gaza is already on the same scale as that seen in the poorer countries of the Southern Sahara, with more than half of all Palestinian families eating only one meal a day.

This was the impact of Israel's unilateral withdrawal, even before Israel's massive bombardment and reinvasion in July 2006 after Hamas militants captured an Israeli soldier.

# 15

## THE PALESTINIAN AND ISRAELI ELECTIONS, 2006

For several reasons, including the Israeli withdrawal of set-tlers from Gaza in August 2005 and the threat of success by Hamas candidates, the scheduled Palestinian parliamentary elections were postponed from July 2005 until January 2006—almost exactly ten years after Yasir Arafat and Legisla-tive Council members first took office. Although the results of previous campaigns had been predictable, the entry of Hamas candidates brought uncertainty and drama to these 132 contests. This time there was an outpouring of interna-tional observers, in addition to our Carter Center–NDI team. In order to obtain approval from Washington, our American delegation had to refrain from meeting with Hamas leaders or candidates—at least prior to the election.

With Ariel Sharon incapacitated by severe illness, Ehud

Olmert was acting as prime minister and the head of Kadima, a new political coalition that was formed when Sharon withdrew from the Likud Party in November 2005. Sharon's purpose was to implement the unilateral disengagement policy and to complete building a wall to separate Palestinians from territory to be claimed by Israel. To distinguish itself from the right-wing Likud Party, Sharon's new organization maintains that "the balance between allowing Jews to fulfill their historic right to live anywhere in the Land of Israel and maintaining the continued existence of Israel as the national Jewish home necessitates a choice that requires territorial compromise." Kadima claims that the advancement of the peace process with the Palestinians is a primary goal: "Israel's existence as the national home of the Jewish people mandates the acceptance of the principle that the end of the conflict will be manifested in the existence of two nation states, based on existing demographic realities, living in peace and security side by side." Sharon positioned the party as a centrist movement that, except for Israel's crippling caveats, supports the Roadmap for Peace.

Because of the strong potential challenge from Hamas, Israeli officials and many Fatah leaders had wanted to postpone or cancel the Palestinian elections. Hamas had not accepted the PLO's commitments at Oslo that recognized the "right of the State of Israel to exist in peace and security" and that renounced the use of terrorism and other acts of violence, but the United States exerted enough pressure to permit the elections to be held. Hamas was now holding many local posts, and their incumbent officials had been free of any allegations of corruption and, for sixteen months, had meticulously observed a cease-fire commitment, which they called *hudna*. Fatah, the party of Arafat and Abbas, had become vulnerable because of its administrative ineffectiveness and alleged corruption. Another factor was that both Israel and the United States had ignored Abbas as an acceptable negotiating partner in the search for peace, publicly branding him (and Fatah) as insignificant.

In preparation for the election, many of Fatah's old-line leaders were replaced by younger candidates loyal to Marwan Barghouti, a militant serving a life sentence in an Israeli prison. He was said to have orchestrated the intifada and also the hudna, and his statements from jail had a great impact. He seemed to be the most popular Fatah leader, and at times it appeared that the Israelis wanted to promote his suggestions, often at the expense of Abbas. They had permitted Barghouti to meet with other prisoners and to be interviewed by news media with global distribution.

Late results from both Israeli and Palestinian pollsters indicated that about 35 percent of the parliamentary seats would go to Hamas candidates. Israel had announced that without a dramatic moderation of its policies, even this involvement by Hamas would preclude any initiation of substantive peace talks between Israelis and Palestinians (already absent for the past five years) and could terminate humanitarian aid and other funds that had been channeled through the Palestinian government.

Shortly after arriving in Israel, Rosalynn and I had an extensive discussion with Acting Prime Minister Ehud Olmert, whom we had known for more than twenty years. He and I have had many arguments (and some agreements) since he was a young Likud parliamentarian, and I've come to appreciate his intelligence, political acumen, personal ambition, and strong will. We considered him to be a formidable leader of the new Kadima Party and, almost certainly, Israel's next prime minister. Current polls showed that Kadima had actually gained support since Olmert replaced Ariel Sharon. He told us that he would continue Sharon's policies and made it plain that he could resume peace talks with Abbas only after *all* radical Palestinian groups were completely disarmed and *all* violent acts were prevented, emphasizing the *all*. I asked if a genuine good-faith effort to control violence would be sufficient, pointing out that *total* peace was a hopeless prospect in any society. He shook his head, with a smile.

The following morning (Monday), I addressed the Herzliya Conference, the foremost annual forum for Israeli and international leaders to express their views concerning the most important current issues. Even though recognizing the conservative makeup of the audience, I expressed my opinions frankly and briefly, emphasizing my role in previous peace efforts, deploring Israel's expansive settlement policy and the intrusive route of the dividing wall, and extolling the Geneva

Initiative as a reasonable basis for peace. Then I answered a series of questions for about half an hour. I had a respectful and polite reception, but I commented in closing that their questions had received more applause than my answers.

We later met with Israeli Foreign Minister Tzipi Livni, Labor Party leader Amir Peretz, Shimon Peres, Quartet special economic envoy James Wolfensohn, a public relations spokesman for Hamas (but not its candidates), candidates of Fatah and independent parties, Yossi Beilin and others who had orchestrated the Geneva Initiative, the U.N. coordinator for Middle East peace, and leaders of the major international election observer groups.

We drove to Ramallah to consult with the leaders of the Central Election Commission and then met with Palestinian President Mahmoud Abbas. Although he expressed confidence in the outcome of the election, he was obviously distressed at having been bypassed or ignored in the "nonexistent peace process." He pointed out that the people of Palestine now had few opportunities for gainful employment or for contact with either Israel or the outside world, that the Palestinian economy was in a shambles, and that Olmert was threatening to withhold about $55 million per month in taxes and customs receipts that were collected on behalf of the Palestinians under an economic protocol signed in 1994. The Palestinian National Authority already had a $900 million deficit and would have difficulty paying its bills or meeting payrolls. He said that Israeli policy had precluded the training and equipping of his security force, so that only 10 percent of its personnel had sidearms or communications equipment.

On election day, Rosalynn and I visited more than two dozen polling sites in East Jerusalem and its outskirts, Hebron, Ramallah, and Jericho. The same rigid restraints were imposed by Israel to minimize voting in East Jerusalem, but otherwise the election was orderly and peaceful. It was obvious to our observers that there was a clear preference for Hamas candidates even in historically strong Fatah communities. Even so, we were all surprised at the size of the Hamas victory. Hamas received a narrow victory in popular votes but won such a clear majority of parliamentary seats (74 of 132) that members of the Fatah government immediately announced their resignation.

I remained for an extra day to assess the situation and to talk with key leaders. In Ramallah I found President Abbas willing to retain his office during the three years remaining in his term but in a quandary about how to deal with the Hamas victory, the formation of a new government, the near-bankruptcy of the Palestinian National Authority, and uncertainty about Israeli policies. He was proud of the honest, fair, and safe election process. Hamas leaders had expressed their desire to form a unity government with Fatah and the smaller independent parties, but Abbas's intention was not to cooperate with them, and he resisted my urging him to reconsider.

The Fatah leader was not prepared to acknowledge the allegations of corruption that were a significant cause of the Hamas success, but he pointed out that one of the major factors in the voting had been his apparent ineffectiveness because he had been ignored by Israel and the Quartet leaders. There had been a few token meetings during his first year as president, but he said that neither the United States nor Israel was prepared for substantive peace talks, using the unilateral withdrawal from Gaza as an excuse. He reminded me that there had been no opportunity for a Palestinian leader to participate in peace talks for the past five years, as the Israelis confiscated more and more land in the West Bank and imposed increasingly severe restrictions on his people. Israel had taken more control of the consumer and production sectors of the area's economy, making it an exclusive market for many Israeli products even among the local Palestinian citizens, who could not sell their own products in Israel, Jordan, or other places.

Abbas said that despite the conduct of exemplary democratic elections, the Palestinians had never had an opportunity to forge a viable government. Their economic system had been forced back into the preindustrial age and their territory broken into ever-smaller fragments. Abbas informed me that there were not enough funds available to meet his February payroll for police, teachers, nurses, and other service providers, and any reduction in their income because of the election results would be disastrous.

Although I had had no direct contact with Hamas since Arafat's election as president and had pledged to refrain from meeting with them until after this recent election, I decided that it was time for me to consult with them again. In The Carter Center's Ramallah office set up to monitor the election, I talked to Hamas member Dr. Mahmoud Ramahi, an anesthesiologist who reminded me that I had met with him ten years earlier. He was later chosen as the legislature's secretary and a spokesperson for Hamas in the West Bank. (Along with some other Hamas legislators who live in the West Bank, he is now imprisoned by the Israelis.)

When I questioned him about the necessity for Hamas to renounce violence and recognize Israel, he responded that they had not committed an act of violence since a cease-fire was declared in August 2004 and were willing and able to extend and enforce their cease-fire (hudna) for "two, ten, or fifty years"—if Israel would reciprocate by refraining from attacks on Palestinians. He added that there had been no allegations of terrorism or corruption among their serving local leaders, and that Israel had so far refused to recognize the Palestinian National Authority (only the PLO) and had rejected the key provisions of the Oslo Agreement. Hamas's first priorities would be to form a government, to maintain order, and to deal with the financial crisis.

He also asked, "Where is the Israel you would have us recognize? Does it include the West Bank and East Jerusalem?" He added that they would have no need to relate directly to the Israelis but wanted a reciprocal cease-fire to be maintained. He hoped that Fatah would join in the new government and that Abbas would continue to serve as its president and to handle all foreign affairs. Their future actions would, of course, reveal their true commitments, but my guess was that during the immediate future they wanted to consolidate their political gains, maintain domestic order and stability, and refrain from any contacts with Israel. It would be a tragedy—especially for the Palestinians—if they decided to promote or condone terrorism.

During the next few weeks Hamas attempted unsuccessfully to induce Fatah members to take some of the cabinet positions and finally proposed its own list, which President Abbas accepted. The most important posts would be held by Dr. Ismail Haniyeh as prime minister, Dr. Mahmoud al-Zahar as foreign minister, and Speaker of the Assembly Dr. Aziz Dweik, who earned his doctorate at the University of Pennsylvania. A postelection public opinion poll indicated that 73 percent of Palestinians expressed their support for the two-state peace process with Israel, but most felt that Hamas should refrain from recognizing Israel until some of the final status issues were resolved. Only 1 percent of the people were in favor of Hamas's imposing Islamic law in Palestine. Equally encouraging was the result of a March 2006 opinion poll by the Truman Research Institute at Hebrew University revealing that 62 percent of Israelis favored direct talks with Hamas.

The January 2006 election of a Hamas government raised the large and unresolved question of whether Palestinians would continue their policy of rejection of Israel pending a total restoration of their homeland. As president and as head of the PLO, Mahmoud Abbas has made it clear that there is still an opportunity to find a path to permanent peace in the Holy Land through direct talks with Israel. Palestinian Prime Minister Haniyeh announced that his Hamas government was "ready for a dialogue" with the members of the Quartet, expressed approval for direct Olmert-Abbas peace talks, and said that Hamas would change its rejectionist position if a satisfactory agreement could be consummated and approved by the Palestinian people. Such Palestinian approval of a final peace agreement was an important facet of the Camp David Accords.

Although there was still a wide difference in the prerequisites for talks, news analysts welcomed what seemed to be a more moderate Palestinian position. The U.S. response was that Hamas must first recognize Israel, renounce violence, and agree to honor previously negotiated agreements. Israel's response, delivered by its defense minister, was that all seventy-four Hamas members of the parliament would be targeted for assassination in case of another violent attack on Israelis by any Palestinian.

Some Palestinian intellectuals tell me that a Hamas-influenced PLO could be more capable of modest compromises on such cardinal issues as Jerusalem, Palestinian refugees, and Jewish settlements in the West Bank. With a single-mindedness amounting to tunnel vision, Palestinians see the restoration of their rights, defined by international law, as the key to peace throughout the broader Middle East, including the Gulf states.

It should be remembered that Mahmoud Abbas is not only the president of the Palestinian National Authority, with substantial authority under Palestinian law, but the undisputed leader of the PLO, the only Palestinian entity recognized by Israel or the international community. He has publicly endorsed the international community's Roadmap for Peace without equivocation and has been eager to negotiate with Israel since first becoming prime minister three years before being elected president.

It is certainly possible that the path of the Palestinians is leading to a dead end, and that even their Arab allies will tire of actively supporting the Palestinian cause. Martin Luther King, Jr., once said that nothing would hurt the black cause in America more than for whites simply to grow bored with it. Nor is Palestinian willingness to resort to violence likely to be any more fruitful in the future than it has been in the past. It must be noted that by following policies of confrontation and inflexibility, Palestinians have alienated many moderate leaders in Israel and America and have not regained any of their territory or other basic rights.

The fate of all Palestinians depends on whether those in the occupied territories choose to pursue their goals by peaceful means or by continued bloodshed. A genuine move toward peace might bring rich dividends by arousing support in the United States and other nations.

At about the same time as the Hamas government was formed late in March 2006, a small turnout of Israeli citizens divided their support so that among the 120 seats in the Knesset, the new Kadima Party had a disappointing 29 seats, Labor 20, Likud 12, Shas 12, and minor parties shared the other 47. At one time, Kadima had been expected to gain 43 seats based on its pledge of a unilateral expansion to the "great wall." The results showed an electorate more divided concerning the acceptance of this plan than had been expected, and they indicated some lack of confidence in Olmert as Israel's prime minister. No Arab-Israeli members are included among the twenty-five members of the cabinet.

# 16

---◆---

# THE WALL AS A PRISON

With increasing control of East Jerusalem, with relative security from the wall surrounding what is left of the West Bank, and with thousands of remaining settlers east of the wall protected by a strong occupying force, there is a temptation for some Israelis simply to avoid any further efforts to seek a peace agreement based on the Quartet's Roadmap or good-faith negotiations on any other basis.

In this diplomatic vacuum, Israeli leaders have embarked on a series of unilateral decisions, bypassing both Washington and the Palestinians. Their presumption is that an encircling barrier will finally resolve the Palestinian problem. Utilizing their political and military dominance, they are imposing a system of partial withdrawal, encapsulation, and apartheid on the Muslim and Christian citizens of the occupied territories. The driving purpose for the forced separation of the two peoples is unlike that in South Africa—not racism, but the acquisition of land. There has been a determined and remarkably effective effort to isolate settlers from Palestinians, so that a Jewish family can commute from Jerusalem to their highly subsidized home deep in the West Bank on roads from which others are excluded, without ever coming in contact with any facet of Arab life.

Withdrawal from Gaza was the first unilateral step, leaving a tiny and nonviable economic and political entity, circumscribed and isolated, with no dependable access to the air, sea, or even other Palestinians. The future prospects for the West Bank are even more dismal. Especially troublesome is the huge dividing wall in populated areas and an impassable fence in rural areas. The status of this barrier is a key to future peace in the Middle East. The original idea of a physical obstruction was promoted by Israeli moderates as a means of preventing intrusive attacks after the withdrawal of Israel's occupation forces. The first barrier, surrounding Gaza, proved that this was a valid premise, in that there was a substantial decrease in cross-border raids. The plan was to continue construction of the barricade along the border between Israel and the West Bank.

Instead, the governments of Ariel Sharon and Ehud Olmert have built the fence and wall mainly within Palestinian territory, intruding deeply into the West Bank to encompass Israeli settlement blocs and large areas of other Palestinian land. It is projected to be at least three and a half times as long as Israel's internationally recognized border

# Map 9

Palestinians
Surrounded
2006

Nazareth•

Jenin•

Netanya•

Nablus•

Tel Aviv•

WEST BANK

Mediterranean Sea

Ramallah•

Jerusalem★

N
W    E
S

ISRAEL

•Hebron

Dead
Sea

Gaza•

GAZA
STRIP

Rafah

•Beersheba

JORDAN

Jordan River

EGYPT

NEGEV

West Bank Boundary

Completed Segregation
Wall (April 2006)

Proposed Segregation
Wall Route

Area of Planned Israeli
Settlement Control

▲  Permanent Settlements
from the Olmert Plan

0      10      20 miles
0    10    20 kilometers

and already cuts directly through Palestinian villages, divides families from their gardens and farmland, and includes 375,000 Palestinians on the "Israeli" side of the wall, 175,000 of whom are outside Jerusalem. One example is that the wandering wall almost completely surrounds the Palestinian city of Qalqiliya with its 45,000 inhabitants, with most of the citizens' land and about one-third of their water supply confiscated by the Israelis. Almost the same encirclement has occurred around 170,000 citizens of Bethlehem, the birthplace of Jesus.

First, a wide swath must be bulldozed through communities before the wall can be built. In addition to the concrete and electrified fencing materials used in the construction, the barrier includes two-meter-deep trenches, roads for patrol vehicles, electronic ground and fence sensors, thermal imaging and video cameras, sniper towers, and razor wire—almost entirely on Palestinian land. The area between the segregation barrier and the Israeli border has been designated a closed military region for an indefinite period of time. Israeli directives state that every Palestinian over the age of twelve living in the closed area has to obtain a "permanent resident permit" from the civil administration to enable them to continue to live in their own homes. They are considered to be aliens, without the rights of Israeli citizens.

To summarize, whatever territory Israel decides to confiscate will be on its side of the wall, but Israelis will still retain control of the Palestinians who will be on the other side of the barrier, enclosed between it and Israel's forces in the Jordan River valley.

President George W. Bush said, "I think the wall is a problem. It is very difficult to develop confidence between the Palestinians and the Israelis with a wall snaking through the West Bank." Since 1945, the International Court of Justice has functioned essentially as the judicial arm of the United Nations system, and in July 2004 the court determined that the Israeli government's construction of the segregation wall in the occupied Palestinian West Bank was illegal. Even Thomas Buergenthal, the American judge who cast the lone negative vote (largely on procedural grounds), acknowledged that the Palestinians were under occupation and had the right to self-determination, that Israel was obligated to adhere to international humanitarian law, and that there were serious questions whether routing an impenetrable barrier to protect West Bank settlements would qualify as legitimate self-defense.

The court acknowledged Israel's right to protect the lives of its citizens by building a protective barrier within its own national border but based its negative ruling on international law including the Fourth Geneva Convention, which forbids an occupying power from transferring any parts of its civilian population into territories seized by military force. The court called on Israel to cease construction of the wall, to dismantle what has already been built in areas within the occupied Palestinian territory, and to compensate Palestinians who have suffered losses as a result of the wall's construction. The Israeli Supreme Court has chosen not to accept the International Court's decision but acknowledged that Israel holds the West Bank "in belligerent occupation" and that "the law of belligerent occupation . . . imposes conditions" on the authority of the military, even in areas related to security.

The wall ravages many places along its devious route that are important to Christians. In addition to enclosing Bethlehem in one of its most notable intrusions, an especially heartbreaking division is on the southern slope of the Mount of Olives, a favorite place for Jesus and his disciples, and very near Bethany, where they often visited Mary, Martha, and their brother, Lazarus. There is a church named for one of the sisters, Santa Marta Monastery, where Israel's thirty-foot concrete wall cuts through the property. The house of worship is now on the Jerusalem side, and its parishioners are separated from it because they cannot get permits to enter Jerusalem. Its priest, Father Claudio Ghilardi, says, "For nine hundred years we have lived here under Turkish, British, Jordanian, and Israeli governments, and no one has ever stopped people coming to pray. It is scandalous. This is not a barrier. It is a border. Why don't they speak the truth?"

Countering Israeli arguments that the wall is to keep Palestinian suicide bombers from Israel, Father Claudio adds a comment that describes the path of the entire barrier: "The Wall is not separating Palestinians from Jews; rather, Palestinians from Palestinians." Nearby are three convents that will also be cut off from the people they serve. These 2,000 Palestinian Christians have lost their place of worship and their spiritual center.

In addition to cutting off about 200,000 Palestinians in Jerusalem from their relatives, property, schools, and businesses, the wall is designed to complete the enclosure of a severely truncated Palestine, a small portion of its original size, compartmentalized, divided into cantons, occupied by Israeli security forces, and isolated from the outside world. In addition, a network of exclusive highways is being built across even these fragments of the West Bank to connect the new Greater Israel in the west with the occupied Jordan River valley in the east, where 7,000 Jews are living in twenty-one heavily protected settlements among about 50,000 Palestinians who are still permitted to stay there. The area along the Jordan River, which is now planned as the eastern leg of the encirclement of the Palestinians, is one of Palestine's most lucrative and productive agricultural regions. Most of its inhabitants were forcibly evicted in 1967, and the Israelis have not allowed these original families to return. Israeli customs officers keep lists of their names and are careful to prohibit their crossing any international checkpoint into the occupied territory, where they might lay claim to their homes and farmland.*

---

*The best description of the barrier, its routing and impact, is shown in the film *The Iron Wall*, produced by the Palestinian Agricultural Relief Committees. It is available for $10 from PARC, at www.theironwall.ps/.

It is obvious that the Palestinians will be left with no territory in which to establish a viable state, but completely enclosed within the barrier and the occupied Jordan River valley. The Palestinians will have a future impossible for them or any responsible portion of the international community to accept, and Israel's permanent status will be increasingly troubled and uncertain as deprived people fight oppression and the relative number of Jewish citizens decreases demographically (compared to Arabs) both within Israel and in Palestine. This prospect is clear to most Israelis, who also view it as a distortion of their values. Recent events involving Gaza and Lebanon demonstrate the inevitable escalation in tension and violence within Palestine and stronger resentment and animosity from the world community against both Israel and America.

One of the vulnerabilities of Israel and a potential cause of violence is the holding of prisoners. Militant Palestinians and Lebanese know that a captured Israeli soldier or civilian is either a valuable bargaining chip for prisoner exchange or a cause of conflict. There have been several such trades: 1,150 Palestinians for three Israelis in 1985; 123 Lebanese for the remains of two Israeli soldiers in 1996; and 433 Palestinians and others for an Israeli businessman and the remains of three soldiers in 2004.

International human rights organizations estimate that since 1967 more than 630,000 Palestinians (about 20 percent of the total population) in the occupied territories have been detained at some time by the Israelis, arousing deep resentment among the families involved. Although the vast majority of prisoners are men, there are a large number of women and children being held. Between the ages of twelve and fourteen, children can be sentenced for a period of up to six months, and after the age of fourteen Palestinian children are tried as adults, a violation of international law.

In addition to time in jail, the pretrial periods can be quite lengthy. Under special Israeli laws covering the period before sentencing, Palestinian detainees can be interrogated for a total period of 180 days and denied lawyer visits for intervals of 90 days. "Administrative detention" is indefinitely renewable under military regulations. Confessions extracted through torture are admissible in Israeli courts. Accused persons usually are tried in military courts in the West Bank, and then incarcerated in prisons inside Israel. This means that both family visits and access to lawyers are prohibited during the frequent and extended times of tight travel restrictions. The Fourth Geneva Convention prohibits this policy, stating: "Protected persons accused of offences shall be detained in the occupied country, and if convicted they shall serve their sentences therein."

The cycle of violence erupted once more in June 2006, when Palestinians dug a tunnel under the barrier that surrounds Gaza and attacked some Israeli soldiers, capturing one of them. They offered to exchange the soldier for the release of some of the 95 women and 313 children who are among about

8,500 Palestinians in Israeli prisons. Israel rejected any negotiations and, in an attempt to rescue the soldier and to stop the firing of homemade rockets into Israeli territory, invaded parts of Gaza, bombing government buildings and destroying connecting bridges and the power station that provides electricity and water. There were heavy casualties and Gaza was even more isolated. When Hamas and Fatah leaders agreed to accept a proposal from the revered prisoner, Marwan Barghouti, as a demonstration of their unity, Israel responded by seizing 64 members of Hamas in the West Bank, including a third of the Palestinian cabinet and 23 legislators. Israeli officials announced that they would be imprisoned until military tribunals could decide what additional punishment would be imposed. At the end of August, the deputy prime minister and six other cabinet officers plus thirty members of the Legislative Council were being held, including the speaker of the parliament, Aziz Dweik.

Claiming to be supporting the beleaguered Palestinians, Hezbollah militants based in Lebanon attacked Israeli patrol vehicles in Israel, killing three Israeli soldiers and capturing two others. Prime Minister Olmert announced that this was a national declaration of war, then imposed a naval blockade and launched attacks on multiple targets in Beirut and throughout Southern Lebanon. Hezbollah leaders demanded the release of Lebanese prisoners and the withdrawal of Israel from the disputed area of Shebaa Farms, and Hezbollah launched a barrage of rockets on cities in northern Israel.

During the first month of fighting, more than 800 Lebanese civilians were dead or missing under rubble and a million—one-fourth of the population—were displaced. Twenty-seven Israeli civilians were killed, and a large number left their homes in northern Israel or lived in bomb shelters to escape the bombardment of Hezbollah rockets. There were also an unknown number of military casualties on both sides.

Although many Lebanese condemned the strength and provocative acts of Hezbollah in Southern Lebanon, the nation's leaders soon formed a united front in response to Israeli attacks. Lebanese Prime Minister Fouad Siniora repeatedly called for a cease-fire and assistance for his country, saying, "The country has been torn to shreds. Lebanon deserves life." Commenting on the U.S.–Israeli opposition to an immediate cease-fire, he quoted the historian Tacitus of ancient Rome: "They created desolation and call it peace." Saad Hariri, whose father was prime minister and believed to have been assassinated by friends of Syria, cried out, "What are the United States and Israel doing? You promote democracy and then you allow it to be destroyed."

This cycle of provocative acts by Arab militants and the devastating military response by Israel demonstrates once more the permanent, festering results of the unresolved Middle East dispute. Israel's powerful military force can, with American acquiescence or support, destroy the economic infrastructure and inflict heavy casualties in Gaza, Lebanon, and even other nations. But when this devastation occurs, guerrilla movements are likely to survive, becoming more united and marshaling wider support.

A poll by the Beirut Center for Research and Information after three weeks of Israeli bombing found that 87 percent of Lebanese supported Hezbollah's battles with Israel. This included 80 percent of Lebanese Christians, who are normally inclined to be friendly to Israel and politically opposed to militant Muslims.

For five weeks, the United States government strongly supported Israel, encouraged their bombardment of Lebanon, and blocked the efforts of France and other nations to impose an immediate cease-fire. The issues involved cessation of all combat, disarming of Hezbollah, withdrawal of Israeli forces from all of Lebanon including Shebaa Farms, the exchange of prisoners, and an international peacekeeping force to be established as a buffer. Finally, on August 11, the United Nations Security Council passed resolution 1701, which provided that combat would cease and that 15,000 Lebanese troops and an equal number from the international community would be deployed in Southern Lebanon as both Israeli and Hezbollah military forces withdrew. The key issues of prisoner exchange, Israel's occupation of Shebaa Farms, and the disarming of Hezbollah were postponed, while Israel continued its pounding of the Palestinians in Gaza. While the world's attention was focused on the Israel-Lebanon conflict, more than 400 Palestinians, 75 of them children, were killed in Gaza, while three Israeli soldiers lost their lives.

What were the causes and results of the Israeli-Lebanese war? The conflict began when Hezbollah militants attacked two Israeli vehicles, killing three soldiers and capturing two others. Their announced goal was to give support to the Palestinians under attack in Gaza, to force Israel out of the disputed area, and to exchange the captured soldiers for some of the Lebanese prisoners as had been done several times in the past. Israel rejected these demands, surprisingly declared that it had been assaulted by the entire nation of Lebanon, and launched an aerial bombardment that eventually included 7,000 targets throughout the country. Hezbollah responded by firing almost 4,000 rockets into northern Israel.

Who were the losers and winners? Although both sides claimed victory, it is obvious that the greatest losers were the Lebanese and Israeli families who lost lives in aerial strikes from bombs, missiles, and rockets. Many areas of Lebanon were devastated. There were wide-ranging recriminations in Israel against its government leaders who wrought such great destruction and still failed to subdue the Hezbollah militants. American leaders were condemned almost universally for overtly encouraging and supplying weapons for the Israeli attack and for delaying a cease-fire that could have ended the carnage.

Although condemned at first by moderate Arabs for precipitating the confrontation with Israel, Hezbollah gained almost universal Arab support and a propaganda victory for "defending" Lebanon, withstanding the Israeli ground and air attack, and subsequently providing massive sums for repairing damage. Israel's outgoing head of military intelligence, Brigadier General Yossi Kuperwasser, stated that the Hezbollah leader, Sheik Hassan Nasrallah, had played brilliantly on the sense of honor that is so important for many Arabs and Muslims. His message, said Kuperwasser, was "to regain lost pride . . . by readiness to sacrifice, readiness to suffer."

Tragically, this conflict was just another in the repetitive cycle of violence that results from the absence of a comprehensive settlement in the Middle East, exacerbated by the almost unprecedented six-year absence of any real effort to achieve such a goal. Temporary cease-fires and international peacekeeping forces in Lebanon and other troubled areas are just Band-Aids. The root causes of the conflict—occupation of Arab land, mistreatment of the Palestinians, and acceptance of Israel within its legal borders—are yet to be addressed. In fact, Israeli Prime Minister Ehud Olmert authorized construction bids in September for another 690 homes in the occupied West Bank, despite criticism from the White House and leaders of his own government. He also rejected an offer from U.N. Secretary-General Kofi Annan to negotiate an exchange of prisoners.

Leaders on both sides ignore strong majorities that crave peace, allowing extremist-led violence to preempt all opportunities for building a political consensus. A major impediment to progress is Washington's strange policy that dialogue on controversial issues is a privilege to be extended only as a reward for subservient behavior and withheld from those who reject U.S. demands. Direct engagement with Palestinian leader Mahmoud Abbas and government leaders in Damascus will be necessary if negotiated settlements are to be achieved. Failure to address the issues and other key leaders risks the creation of an arc of even greater instability running from Jerusalem through Beirut, Damascus, Baghdad, and Tehran.

A survey by the Pew Center's Global Attitudes Project released in June found that Muslim opinions about the West had worsened drastically, with the Israel-Palestinian issue having become the principal fault line in world conflict.

A notable and promising development, concealed by the conflict in Lebanon, was the agreement (later delayed) between Palestinian leaders of Fatah, Hamas, and some smaller groups to adopt the "National Conciliation Document" that was forged by Marwan Barghouti and other Palestinian prisoners. There is a good prospect that this will lead to a unity government including representatives from the major parties, which would also meet the international community's conditions for lifting the embargo that has been placed on the Palestinian people. This would include the acceptance of a two-state solution, recognition of Israel, and a long-term cease-fire by Hamas if reciprocated by Israel. The Hamas prime minister, Ismail Haniyeh, stated in June, "We have no problem with a sovereign Palestinian state over all our lands within the 1967 borders, living in calm."

# 17

## SUMMARY

Since the Israeli-Egyptian peace treaty was signed in 1979, much blood has been shed unnecessarily and repeated efforts for a negotiated peace between Israel and her neighbors have failed. Despite its criticism from some Arab sources, this treaty stands as proof that diplomacy can bring lasting peace between ancient adversaries. Although disparities among them are often emphasized, the 1974 Israeli-Syrian withdrawal agreement, the 1978 Camp David Accords, the Reagan statement of 1982, the 1993 Oslo Agreement, the treaty between Israel and Jordan in 1994, the Arab peace proposal of 2002, the 2003 Geneva Initiative, and the International Quartet's Roadmap all contain key common elements that can be consolidated if pursued in good faith.

There are two interrelated obstacles to permanent peace in the Middle East:

1. Some Israelis believe they have the right to confiscate and colonize Arab land and try to justify the sustained subjugation and persecution of increasingly hopeless and aggravated Palestinians; and

2. Some Palestinians react by honoring suicide bombers as martyrs to be rewarded in heaven and consider the killing of Israelis as victories.

In turn, Israel responds with retribution and oppression, and militant Palestinians refuse to recognize the legitimacy of Israel and vow to destroy the nation. The cycle of distrust and violence is sustained, and efforts for peace are frustrated. Casualties have been high as the occupying forces impose ever tighter controls. From September 2000 until March 2006, 3,982 Palestinians and 1,084 Israelis were killed in the second intifada, and these numbers include many children: 708 Palestinians and 123 Israelis. As indicated earlier, there was an ever-rising toll of dead and wounded from the latest outbreak of violence in Gaza and Lebanon.

The only rational response to this continuing tragedy is to revitalize the peace process through negotiations between Israelis and Palestinians, but the United States has, in effect, abandoned this effort. It may be that one of the periodic escalations in violence will lead to strong influence being exerted from the International Quartet to implement its Roadmap for Peace. These are the key requirements:

**a. The security of Israel must be guaranteed.** The Arabs must acknowledge openly and specifically that Israel is a reality and has a right to exist in peace, behind secure and recognized borders, and with a firm Arab pledge to terminate any further acts of violence against the legally constituted nation of Israel.

**b. The internal debate within Israel must be resolved in order to define Israel's permanent legal boundary.** The unwavering official policy of the United States since Israel became a state has been that its borders, unless modified through negotiations, must coincide with the armistice lines prevailing from 1949 until 1967. The unanimously adopted U.N. Resolution 242 specifies the withdrawal of Israeli armed forces from occupied territories. This obligation was reconfirmed by Israel's leaders in agreements negotiated in 1978 at Camp David and in 1993 at Oslo, for which they received the Nobel Peace Prize, and both of these commitments were officially ratified by the Israeli government. Also, as a member of the International Quartet that includes Russia, the United Nations, and the European Union, America supports the Roadmap for Peace, which espouses exactly the same requirements. Palestinian leaders unequivocally accepted this proposal, but Israel has officially rejected its key provisions with unacceptable caveats and prerequisites.

Despite these recent developments, it is encouraging that Israel has made previous commitments to peace as confirmed by the Camp David Accords, the withdrawal of its forces from the Sinai, the more recent movement of settlers from Gaza, and its official endorsement of pertinent U.N. resolutions. After the Six-Day War in 1967, Israeli military forces occupied all of the territory indicated on Map 4, but joined the United States and other nations in supporting United Nations Resolution 242, which is still the binding law that condemns the acquisition of land by force and requires Israeli withdrawal from occupied territories.

**c. The sovereignty of all Middle East nations and sanctity of international borders must be honored.** There is little doubt that accommodation with Palestinians can bring full Arab recognition of Israel and its right to live in peace, with an Arab commitment to restrain further violence initiated by extremist Palestinians.

The overriding problem is that, for more than a quarter century, the actions of some Israeli leaders have been in direct conflict with the official policies of the United States, the international community, and their own negotiated agreements. Regardless of whether Palestinians had no formalized government, one headed by Yasir Arafat or Mahmoud Abbas, or one with Abbas as president and Hamas controlling the parliament and cabinet, Israel's continued control and colonization of Palestinian land have been the primary obstacles to a comprehensive peace agreement in the Holy Land. In order to perpetuate the occupation, Israeli forces have deprived their unwilling subjects of basic human rights. No objective person could personally observe existing conditions in the West Bank and dispute these statements.

Two other interrelated factors have contributed to the perpetuation of violence and regional upheaval: the condoning of illegal Israeli actions from a submissive White House and U.S. Congress during recent years, and the deference with which other international leaders permit this unofficial U.S. policy in the Middle East to prevail. There are constant and vehement political and media debates in Israel concerning its policies in the West Bank, but because of powerful political, economic, and religious forces in the United States, Israeli government decisions are rarely questioned or condemned, voices from Jerusalem dominate in our media, and most American citizens are unaware of circumstances in the occupied territories. At the same time, political leaders and news media in Europe are highly critical of Israeli policies, affecting public attitudes. Americans were surprised and angered by an opinion poll, published by the *International Herald Tribune* in October 2003, of 7,500 citizens in fifteen European nations, indicating that Israel was considered to be the top threat to world peace, ahead of North Korea, Iran, or Afghanistan.

The United States has used its U.N. Security Council veto more than forty times to block resolutions critical of Israel. Some of these vetoes have brought international discredit on the United States, and there is little doubt that the lack of a persistent effort to resolve the Palestinian issue is a major source of anti-American sentiment and terrorist activity throughout the Middle East and the Islamic world.

A new factor in the region is that the Palestinian election of January 2006 gave Hamas members control of the parliament and a cabinet headed by the prime minister. Israel and the United States reacted by announcing a policy of isolating and destabilizing the new government. Elected officials are denied travel permits to participate in parliamentary affairs, Gaza is effectively isolated, and every effort is made to block humanitarian funds to Palestinians, to prevent their right to employment or commercial trade, and to deny them access to Israel and the outside world.

In order to achieve its goals, Israel has decided to avoid any peace negotiations and to escape even the mild restraints of the United States by taking unilateral action, called "convergence" or "realignment," to carve out for itself the choice portions of the West Bank, leaving Palestinians destitute within a small and fragmented remnant of their own land. The holding of almost 10,000 Arab prisoners and the destructive military response to the capture of three Israeli soldiers have aroused global concern about the hair-trigger possibility of a regional war being launched.

Despite these immediate challenges, we must not assume that the future is hopeless. Down through the years I have seen despair and frustration evolve into optimism and progress and, even now, we must not abandon efforts to achieve permanent peace for Israelis and freedom and justice for Palestinians. There are some positive factors on which we may rely.

As I said in a 1979 speech to the Israeli Knesset, "The people support a settlement. Political leaders are the obstacles to peace." Over the years, public opinion surveys have consistently shown that a majority of Israelis favor withdrawing from Palestinian territory in exchange for peace ("swapping land for peace"), and recent polls show that 80 percent of Palestinians still want a two-state peace agreement with Israel, with nearly 70 percent supporting the moderate Mahmoud Abbas as their president and spokesman.

There have been some other encouraging developments over the years. Along with the awareness among most Israelis that a solution to the Palestinian question is critical if there is ever to be a comprehensive settlement, there is a growing recognition in the Arab world that Israel is an unchanging reality. Most Palestinians and other Arabs maintain that the proposal made by Saudi Arabia's King Abdullah, a proposal approved at the Arab summit in 2002 (Appendix 6), is a public acknowledgment of Israel's right to exist within its legal borders and shows willingness to work out disputes that have so far not been addressed directly. The Delphic wording of this statement was deliberate, in Arabic as well as in Hebrew and English, but the Arabs defend it by saying it is there to be explored by the Israelis and others and that, in any case, it is a more positive and clear commitment to international law than anything now coming from Israel.

Furthermore, the remaining differences and their potential resolution are clearly defined. Both Israel and the Arab countries have endorsed the crucial and unavoidable U.N. Resolutions 242 and 338, under which peace agreements have already been evolved.

Here are two voices, one Palestinian and the other Israeli, with remarkably similar assessments of what needs to be done.

Jonathan Kuttab, Palestinian human rights lawyer: "Everybody knows what it will take to achieve a permanent and lasting peace that addresses the basic interests of both sides: It's a two-state solution. It's withdrawal to 1967 borders. It's dismantlement of the settlements. It's some kind of shared status for a united Jerusalem, the capital of both parties. The West Bank and Gaza would have to be demilitarized to remove any security threats to Israel. Some kind of solution would have to be reached for the refugee problem, some qualified right of return, with compensation. Everyone knows the solution; the question is: Is there political will to implement it?"

Dr. Naomi Chazan, professor at Hebrew University and former deputy speaker of the Israeli Knesset: "I don't think any difference now remains between the majority of Israelis and Palestinians in understanding that there has to be some kind of accommodation between both people. There are two possibilities on how to do it. To acknowledge and then to implement the Palestine right to self-determination, and to make sure that the two-state solution is a just and fair solution, allowing for the creation of a viable state alongside Israel on the 1967 boundaries, and if there are any changes, they are by agreement on a swap basis. And on the Israeli side, there is the need to maintain a democratic state with a Jewish majority, which can only be achieved through the creation of a Palestinian state alongside Israel."

An important fact to remember is that President Mahmoud Abbas retains all presidential authority that was exercised by Yasir Arafat when he negotiated the Oslo Agreement, and the Hamas prime minister has stated that his government supports peace talks between Israel and Abbas. He added that Hamas would modify its rejection of Israel if there is a negotiated agreement that Palestinians can approve (as specified in the Camp David Accords). It is imperative that the general Arab community and all significant Palestinian groups make it clear that they renounce all acts of violence against innocent civilians and will accept international laws, the Arab peace proposal of 2002, and the ultimate goals of the Roadmap for Peace.

One promising development came in May 2006 when Marwan Barghouti, the most popular and influential leader of Fatah, joined forces in an Israeli prison with Abed al-Halak Natashe, a trusted spokesman for Hamas, in endorsing a two-state proposal that could unite the two Palestinian factions.

Their influence is enormous. The prisoners' proposal called for a unity government with Hamas joining the PLO, the release of all political prisoners, acceptance of Israel as a neighbor within its legal borders, and an end to violent acts within Israel (but not in Palestinian territory). It endorsed the key U.N. resolutions regarding legal borders and the right of return.

With public opinion polls indicating a 77 percent rate of approval, President Abbas first proposed a referendum among Palestinians on the prisoners' proposal, and then both Hamas and Fatah accepted its provisions.

Although a clear majority of Israelis are persistently willing to accept terms that are tolerable to most of their Arab neighbors, it is clear that none of the options is attractive for all Israelis:

- A forcible annexation of Palestine and its legal absorption into Israel, which could give large numbers of non-Jewish citizens the right to vote and live as equals under the law. This would directly violate international standards and the Camp David Accords, which are the basis for peace with Egypt. At the same time, non-Jewish citizens would make up a powerful swing vote if other Israelis were divided and would ultimately constitute an outright majority in the new Greater Israel. Israel would be further isolated and condemned by the international

community, with no remaining chance to end
hostilities with any appreciable part of the Arab
world.

- A system of apartheid, with two peoples occupying
  the same land but completely separated from each
  other, with Israelis totally dominant and suppressing
  violence by depriving Palestinians of their basic
  human rights. This is the policy now being
  followed, although many citizens of Israel deride
  the racist connotation of prescribing permanent
  second-class status for the Palestinians. As one
  prominent Israeli stated, "I am afraid that we are
  moving toward a government like that of South
  Africa, with a dual society of Jewish rulers and Arab
  subjects with few rights of citizenship. The West
  Bank is not worth it." An unacceptable modification
  of this choice, now being proposed, is the taking of
  substantial portions of the occupied territory, with
  the remaining Palestinians completely surrounded
  by walls, fences, and Israeli checkpoints, living as
  prisoners within the small portion of land left to
  them.

- Withdrawal to the 1967 border as specified in U.N.
  Resolution 242 and as promised in the Camp David
  Accords and the Oslo Agreement and prescribed in
  the Roadmap of the International Quartet. This is

the most attractive option and the only one that can ultimately be acceptable as a basis for peace. Good-faith negotiations can lead to mutually agreeable exchanges of land, perhaps permitting a significant number of Israeli settlers to remain in their present homes near Jerusalem. One version of this choice was spelled out in the Geneva Initiative.

The bottom line is this: Peace will come to Israel and the Middle East only when the Israeli government is willing to comply with international law, with the Roadmap for Peace, with official American policy, with the wishes of a majority of its own citizens—and honor its own previous commitments—by accepting its legal borders. All Arab neighbors must pledge to honor Israel's right to live in peace under these conditions. The United States is squandering international prestige and goodwill and intensifying global anti-American terrorism by unofficially condoning or abetting the Israeli confiscation and colonization of Palestinian territories.

It will be a tragedy—for the Israelis, the Palestinians, and the world—if peace is rejected and a system of oppression, apartheid, and sustained violence is permitted to prevail.

*Appendix 1*

———•◆•———

# U.N. RESOLUTION 242, 1967

UNITED NATIONS SECURITY COUNCIL
RESOLUTION 242, NOVEMBER 22, 1967

The Security Council,

Expressing its continuing concern with the grave situation in the Middle East,

Emphasizing the inadmissibility of the acquisition of territory by war and the need to work for a just and lasting peace in which every State in the area can live in security,

Emphasizing further that all Member States in their acceptance of the Charter of the United Nations have undertaken a commitment to act in accordance with Article 2 of the Charter,

1. Affirms that the fulfillment of Charter principles requires the establishment of a just and lasting peace in the

Middle East which should include the application of both the following principles:

(i) Withdrawal of Israeli armed forces from territories occupied in the recent conflict;

(ii) Termination of all claims or states of belligerency and respect for and acknowledgment of the sovereignty, territorial integrity and political independence of every State in the area and their right to live in peace within secure and recognized boundaries free from threats or acts of force;

2. Affirms further the necessity

(a) For guaranteeing freedom of navigation through international ways in the area;

(b) For achieving a just settlement of the refugee problem;

(c) For guaranteeing the territorial inviolability and political independence of every State in the area, through measures including the establishment of demilitarized zones;

3. Requests the Secretary-General to designate a Special Representative to proceed to the Middle East to establish and maintain contacts with the States concerned in order to promote agreement and assist efforts to achieve a peaceful and accepted settlement in accordance with the provisions and principles of this resolution.

4. Requests the Secretary-General to report to the Security Council on the progress of the efforts of the Special Representative as soon as possible.

# *Appendix 2*

————•◆•————

# U.N. RESOLUTION 338, 1973

UNITED NATIONS SECURITY COUNCIL
RESOLUTION 338, OCTOBER 21–22, 1973

The Security Council

1.   Calls upon all parties to the present fighting to cease all firing and terminate all military activity immediately, no later than 12 hours after the moment of the adoption of this decision, in the positions they now occupy;

2.   Calls upon the parties concerned to start immediately after the cease-fire the implementation of Security Council Resolution 242 (1967) in all of its parts;

3.   Decides that, immediately and concurrently with the cease-fire, negotiations start between the parties concerned under appropriate auspices aimed at establishing a just and durable peace in the Middle East.

# Appendix 3

——•◆•——

# CAMP DAVID ACCORDS, 1978

## A FRAMEWORK FOR PEACE IN THE MIDDLE EAST AGREED AT CAMP DAVID

### Documents Agreed To at Camp David, September 17, 1978

Muhammad Anwar al-Sadat, President of the Arab Republic of Egypt, and Menachem Begin, Prime Minister of Israel, met with Jimmy Carter, President of the United States of America, at Camp David from September 5 to September 17, 1978, and have agreed on the following framework for peace in the Middle East. They invite other parties to the Arab-Israeli conflict to adhere to it.

PREAMBLE

The search for peace in the Middle East must be guided by the following:

—The agreed basis for a peaceful settlement of the conflict between Israel and its neighbors is United Nations Security Council Resolution 242, in all its parts.*

—After four wars during thirty years, despite intensive human efforts, the Middle East, which is the cradle of civilization and the birthplace of three great religions, does not yet enjoy the blessings of peace. The people of the Middle East yearn for peace so that the vast human and natural resources of the region can be turned to the pursuits of peace and so that this area can become a model for coexistence and cooperation among nations.

—The historic initiative of President Sadat in visiting Jerusalem and the reception accorded to him by the Parliament, government and people of Israel, and the reciprocal visit of Prime Minister Begin to Ismailia, the peace proposals made by both leaders, as well as the warm reception of these missions by the people of both countries, have created an unprecedented opportunity for peace which must not be lost if this generation and future generations are to be spared the tragedies of war.

—The provisions of the Charter of the United Nations and the other accepted norms of international law and legit-

*The text of Resolutions 242 and 338 are annexed to this document.

imacy now provide accepted standards for the conduct of relations among all states.

—To achieve a relationship of peace, in the spirit of Article 2 of the United Nations Charter, future negotiations between Israel and any neighbor prepared to negotiate peace and security with it, are necessary for the purpose of carrying out all the provisions and principles of Resolutions 242 and 338.

—Peace requires respect for the sovereignty, territorial integrity and political independence of every state in the area and their right to live in peace within secure and recognized boundaries free from threats or acts of force. Progress toward that goal can accelerate movement toward a new era of reconciliation in the Middle East marked by cooperation in promoting economic development, in maintaining stability, and in assuring security.

—Security is enhanced by a relationship of peace and by cooperation between nations which enjoy normal relations. In addition, under the terms of peace treaties, the parties can, on the basis of reciprocity, agree to special security arrangements such as demilitarized zones, limited armaments areas, early warning stations, the presence of international forces, liaison, agreed measures for monitoring, and other arrangements that they agree are useful.

FRAMEWORK

Taking these factors into account, the parties are determined to reach a just, comprehensive, and durable settlement of the Middle East conflict through the conclusion of peace treaties based on Security Council Resolutions 242 and 338 in all their parts. Their purpose is to achieve peace and good neighborly relations. They recognize that, for peace to endure, it must involve all those who have been most deeply affected by the conflict. They therefore agree that this framework as appropriate is intended by them to constitute a basis for peace not only between Egypt and Israel, but also between Israel and each of its other neighbors which is prepared to negotiate peace with Israel on this basis. With that objective in mind, they have agreed to proceed as follows:

A. West Bank and Gaza

1. Egypt, Israel, Jordan, and the representatives of the Palestinian people should participate in negotiations on the resolution of the Palestinian problem in all its aspects. To achieve that objective, negotiations relating to the West Bank and Gaza should proceed in three stages:

(a) Egypt and Israel agree that, in order to ensure a peaceful and orderly transfer of authority, and taking into account the security concerns of all the parties, there should be transitional arrangements for the West Bank and Gaza for a period not exceeding five years. In order to provide full autonomy to the inhabitants, under these arrangements the Israeli military government and its civilian administration will be withdrawn as soon as a self-governing authority has been freely elected by the inhabitants of these areas to replace the existing military government. To negotiate the details of a transitional arrangement, the Government of Jordan will be invited to join the negotiations on the basis of this framework. These new arrangements should give due consideration both to the principle of self-government by the inhabitants of these territories and to the legitimate security concerns of the parties involved.

(b)    Egypt, Israel, and Jordan will agree on the modalities for establishing the elected self-governing authority in the West Bank and Gaza. The delegations of Egypt and Jordan may include Palestinians from the West Bank and Gaza or other Palestinians as mutually agreed. The parties will negotiate an agreement which will define the powers and responsibilities of the self-governing authority to be exercised in the West Bank and Gaza. A withdrawal of Israeli armed forces will take place and there will be a redeployment of the remaining Israeli forces into specified security locations. The agreement will also include arrangements for assuring internal and external security and public order. A strong local police force will be established, which may include Jordanian citizens. In addition, Israeli and Jordanian forces will participate in joint patrols and in the manning of control posts to assure the security of the borders.

(c)    When the self-governing authority (administrative council) in the West Bank and Gaza is established and inaugurated, the transitional period of five years will begin. As soon as possible, but not later than the third year after the beginning of the transitional period, negotiations will take place to determine the final status of the West Bank and Gaza and its relationship with its neighbors, and to conclude a peace treaty between Israel and Jordan by the end of the transitional period. These negotiations will be conducted among Egypt, Israel, Jordan, and the elected representatives of the inhabitants of the West Bank and Gaza. Two separate but related committees will be convened, one committee, consisting of representatives of the four parties which will negotiate and agree on the final status of the West Bank and Gaza, and its relationships with its neighbors, and the second committee, consisting of representatives of Israel and representatives of Jordan to be joined by the elected representatives of the inhabitants of the West Bank and Gaza, to negotiate the peace treaty between Israel and Jordan, taking into account the agreement reached on the final status of the West Bank and Gaza. The negotiations shall be based on all the provisions and principles of U.N. Security Council Resolution 242. The negotiations will resolve, among other matters, the location of the boundaries and the nature of the security arrangements. The solution from the negotiations must also recognize the legitimate rights of the Palestinian people and their just requirements. In this way, the Palestinians will participate in the determination of their own future through:

1)    The negotiations among Egypt, Israel, Jordan and the representatives of the inhabitants of the West

Bank and Gaza to agree on the final status of the West Bank and Gaza and other outstanding issues by the end of the transitional period.

2)    Submitting their agreement to a vote by the elected representatives of the inhabitants of the West Bank and Gaza.

3)    Providing for the elected representatives of the inhabitants of the West Bank and Gaza to decide how they shall govern themselves consistent with the provisions of their agreement.

4)    Participating as stated above in the work of the committee negotiating the peace treaty between Israel and Jordan.

2.    All necessary measures will be taken and provisions made to assure the security of Israel and its neighbors during the transitional period and beyond. To assist in providing such security, a strong local police force will be constituted by the self-governing authority. It will be composed of inhabitants of the West Bank and Gaza. The police will maintain continuing liaison on internal security matters with the designated Israeli, Jordanian, and Egyptian officers.

3.    During the transitional period, representatives of Egypt, Israel, Jordan, and the self-governing authority will constitute a continuing committee to decide by agreement on the modalities of admission of persons displaced from the West Bank and Gaza in 1967, together with necessary measures to prevent disruption and disorder.

Other matters of common concern may also be dealt with by this committee.

4.   Egypt and Israel will work with each other and with other interested parties to establish agreed procedures for a prompt, just, and permanent implementation of the resolution of the refugee problem.

B.   Egypt-Israel

1.   Egypt and Israel undertake not to resort to the threat or the use of force to settle disputes. Any disputes shall be settled by peaceful means in accordance with the provisions of Article 33 of the Charter of the United Nations.

2.   In order to achieve peace between them, the parties agree to negotiate in good faith with a goal of concluding within three months from the signing of this Framework a peace treaty between them, while inviting the other parties to the conflict to proceed simultaneously to negotiate and conclude similar peace treaties with a view to achieving a comprehensive peace in the area. The Framework for the Conclusion of a Peace Treaty between Egypt and Israel will govern the peace negotiations between them. The parties will agree on the modalities and the timetable for the implementation of their obligations under the treaty.

C.   Associated Principles

1.   Egypt and Israel state that the principles and provisions described below should apply to peace treaties between Israel and each of its neighbors—Egypt, Jordan, Syria, and Lebanon.

2. Signatories shall establish among themselves relationships normal to states at peace with one another. To this end, they should undertake to abide by all the provisions of the Charter of the United Nations. Steps to be taken in this respect include:

(a) full recognition;

(b) abolishing economic boycotts;

(c) guaranteeing that under their jurisdiction the citizens of the other parties shall enjoy the protection of the due process of law.

3. Signatories should explore possibilities for economic development in the context of final peace treaties, with the objective of contributing to the atmosphere of peace, cooperation, and friendship which is their common goal.

4. Claims Commissions may be established for the mutual settlement of all financial claims.

5. The United States shall be invited to participate in the talks on matters related to the modalities of the implementation of the agreements and working out the timetable for the carrying out of the obligations of the parties.

6. The United Nations Security Council shall be requested to endorse the peace treaties and ensure that their provisions shall not be violated. The permanent members of the Security Council shall be requested to underwrite the peace treaties and ensure respect for their provisions. They

shall also be requested to conform their policies and actions with the undertakings contained in this Framework.

For the Government of the Arab Republic of Egypt:
    A. Sadat

For the Government of Israel:
    M. Begin

Witnessed by:
    Jimmy Carter
    President of the United States of America

———•◆•———

# FRAMEWORK FOR EGYPT-ISRAEL PEACE TREATY, 1978

In order to achieve peace between them, Israel and Egypt agree to negotiate in good faith with a goal of concluding within three months of the signing of this framework a peace treaty between them.

It is agreed that:

The site of the negotiations will be under a United Nations flag at a location or locations to be mutually agreed.

All of the principles of U.N. Resolution 242 will apply in this resolution of the dispute between Israel and Egypt.

Unless otherwise mutually agreed, terms of the peace treaty will be implemented between two and three years after the peace treaty is signed.

The following matters are agreed between the parties:

(a)   the full exercise of Egyptian sovereignty up to the internationally recognized border between Egypt and mandated Palestine;

(b)   the withdrawal of Israeli armed forces from the Sinai;

(c)   the use of airfields left by the Israelis near El Arish, Rafah, Ras en Naqb, and Sharm el Sheikh for civilian purposes only, including possible commercial use by all nations;

(d)   the right of free passage by ships of Israel through the Gulf of Suez and the Suez Canal on the basis of the Constantinople Convention of 1888 applying to all nations; the Strait of Tiran and the Gulf of Aqaba are international waterways to be open to all nations for unimpeded and nonsuspendable freedom of navigation and overflight;

(e)   the construction of a highway between the Sinai and Jordan near Elat with guaranteed free and peaceful passage by Egypt and Jordan; and

(f)   the stationing of military forces listed below.

## Stationing of Forces

A.   No more than one division (mechanized or infantry) of Egyptian armed forces will be stationed within an area lying approximately 50 kilometers (km) east of the Gulf of Suez and the Suez Canal.

B.   Only United Nations forces and civil police equipped with light weapons to perform normal police functions will be stationed within an area lying west of the international border and the Gulf of Aqaba, varying in width from 20 km to 40 km.

C.   In the area within 3 km east of the international border there will be Israeli limited military forces not to exceed four infantry battalions and United Nations observers.

D.   Border patrol units, not to exceed three battalions, will supplement the civil police in maintaining order in the area not included above.

The exact demarcation of the above areas will be as decided during the peace negotiations.

Early warning stations may exist to ensure compliance with the terms of the agreement.

United Nations forces will be stationed:

(a)   in part of the area in the Sinai lying within about 20 km of the Mediterranean Sea and adjacent to the international border, and (b) in the Sharm el Sheikh area to ensure freedom of passage through the Strait of Tiran; and these forces will not be removed unless such removal is approved by the Security Council of the United Nations with a unanimous vote of the five permanent members.

After a peace treaty is signed, and after the interim withdrawal is complete, normal relations will be established between Egypt and Israel, including: full recognition, including diplomatic, economic, and cultural relations; termination of economic boycotts and barriers to the free movement of goods and people; and mutual protection of citizens by the due process of law.

INTERIM WITHDRAWAL

Between three months and nine months after the signing of the peace treaty, all Israeli forces will withdraw east of a line extending from a point east of El Arish to Ras Muhammad, the exact location of this line to be determined by mutual agreement.

For the Government of the Arab Republic of Egypt:
    A. Sadat

For the Government of Israel:
    M. Begin

Witnessed by:
    Jimmy Carter
    President of the United States of America

Note: The texts of the documents were released on September 18.

# Appendix 5

———•◆•———

# U.N. RESOLUTION 465, 1980

UNITED NATIONS SECURITY COUNCIL
RESOLUTION 465, MARCH 1, 1980

The Security Council,

Taking note of the reports of the Commission of the Security Council established under resolution 446 (1979) to examine the situation relating to settlements in the Arab territories occupied since 1967, including Jerusalem, contained in documents S/13450 and Corr. 1 and S/13679,

Taking note also of letters from the Permanent Representative of Jordan (S/13801) and the Permanent Representative of Morocco, Chairman of the Islamic Group (S/13802),

Strongly deploring the refusal by Israel to co-operate with the Commission and regretting its formal rejection of resolutions 446 (1979) and 452 (1979),

Affirming once more that the Fourth Geneva Convention relative to the Protection of Civilian Persons in Time of War of 12 August 1949 is applicable to the Arab territories occupied by Israel since 1967, including Jerusalem,

Deploring the decision of the Government of Israel to officially support Israeli settlement in the Palestinian and other Arab territories occupied since 1967,

Deeply concerned over the practices of the Israeli authorities in implementing that settlement policy in the occupied Arab territories, including Jerusalem, and its consequences for the local Arab and Palestinian population,

Taking into account the need to consider measures for the impartial protection of private and public land and property, and water resources,

Bearing in mind the specific status of Jerusalem and, in particular, the need for protection and preservation of the unique spiritual and religious dimension of the Holy Places in the city,

Drawing attention to the grave consequences which the settlement policy is bound to have on any attempt to reach a comprehensive, just and lasting peace in the Middle East,

Recalling pertinent Security Council resolutions, specifically resolutions 237 (1967) of 14 June 1967, 252 (1968) of 21 May 1968, 267 (1969) of 3 July 1969, 271 (1969) of 15 September 1969 and 298 (1971) of 25 September 1971, as well as the consensus statement made by the President of the Security Council on 11 November 1976,

Having invited Mr. Fahd Qawasmeh, Mayor of Al-Khalil (Hebron), in the occupied territory, to supply it with information pursuant to rule 39 of the provisional rules of procedure,

1. Commends the work done by the Commission in preparing the report contained in document S/13679;

2. Accepts the conclusions and recommendations contained in the above-mentioned report of the Commission;

3. Calls upon all parties, particularly the Government of Israel, to co-operate with the Commission;

4. Strongly deplores the decision of Israel to prohibit the free travel of Mayor Fahd Qawasmeh in order to appear before the Security Council, and requests Israel to permit his free travel to the United Nations headquarters for that purpose;

5. Determines that all measures taken by Israel to change the physical character, demographic composition, institutional structure or status of the Palestinian and other Arab territories occupied since 1967, including Jerusalem, or any part thereof, have no legal validity and that Israel's policy and practices of settling parts of its population and new immigrants in those territories constitute a flagrant violation of the Fourth Geneva Convention relative to the Protection of Civilian Persons in Time of War and also constitute a serious obstruction to achieving a comprehensive, just and lasting peace in the Middle East;

6.  Strongly deplores the continuation and persistence of Israel in pursuing those policies and practices and calls upon the Government and people of Israel to rescind those measures, to dismantle the existing settlements and in particular to cease, on an urgent basis, the establishment, construction and planning of settlements in the Arab territories occupied since 1967, including Jerusalem;

7.  Calls upon all States not to provide Israel with any assistance to be used specifically in connexion with settlements in the occupied territories;

8.  Requests the Commission to continue to examine the situation relating to settlements in the Arab territories occupied since 1967, including Jerusalem, to investigate the reported serious depletion of natural resources, particularly the water resources, with a view to ensuring the protection of those important natural resources of the territories under occupation, and to keep under close scrutiny the implementation of the present resolution;

9.  Requests the Commission to report to the Security Council before 1 September 1980, and decides to convene at the earliest possible date thereafter in order to consider the report and the full implementation of the present resolution.

# Appendix 6

ARAB PEACE PROPOSAL,
2002

## THE ARAB LEAGUE "PEACE PLAN,"
### MARCH 28, 2002

The Council of the League of Arab States at the Summit Level, at its 14th Ordinary Session;

Reaffirming the resolution taken in June 1996 at the Cairo Extraordinary Arab Summit that a just and comprehensive peace in the Middle East is the strategic option of the Arab Countries, to be achieved in accordance with International Legality, and which would require a comparable commitment on the part of the Israeli Government;

Having listened to the statement made by His Royal Highness Prince Abdullah Bin Abdullaziz, the Crown Prince of the Kingdom of Saudi Arabia in which his High-

APPENDIX 6

ness presented his Initiative, calling for full Israeli withdrawal from all the Arab territories occupied since June 1967, in implementation of Security Council Resolutions 242 and 338, reaffirmed by the Madrid Conference of 1991 and the land for peace principle, and Israel's acceptance of an independent Palestinian State, with East Jerusalem as its capital, in return for the establishment of normal relations in the context of a comprehensive peace with Israel;

Emanating from the conviction of the Arab countries that a military solution to the conflict will not achieve peace or provide security for the parties, the council:

1. Requests Israel to reconsider its policies and declare that a just peace is its strategic option as well.

2. Further calls upon Israel to affirm:

a. Full Israeli withdrawal from all the territories occupied since 1967, including the Syrian Golan Heights to the lines of June 4, 1967 as well as the remaining occupied Lebanese territories in the south of Lebanon.

b. Achievement of a just solution to the Palestinian Refugee problem to be agreed upon in accordance with UN General Assembly Resolution 194.

c. The acceptance of the establishment of a Sovereign Independent Palestinian State on the Palestinian territories occupied since the 4th of June 1967 in the West Bank and Gaza Strip, with East Jerusalem as its capital.

3. Consequently, the Arab Countries affirm the following:

a. Consider the Arab-Israeli conflict ended, and enter into a peace agreement with Israel, and provide security for all the states of the region.

b. Establish normal relations with Israel in the context of this comprehensive peace.

4. Assures the rejection of all forms of Palestinian patriation which conflict with the special circumstances of the Arab host countries.

5. Calls upon the government of Israel and all Israelis to accept this initiative in order to safeguard the prospects for peace and stop the further shedding of blood, enabling the Arab countries and Israel to live in peace and good neighbourliness and provide future generations with security, stability and prosperity.

6. Invites the international community and all countries and organisations to support this initiative.

7. Requests the chairman of the summit to form a special committee composed of some of its concerned member states and the secretary general of the League of Arab States to pursue the necessary contacts to gain support for this initiative at all levels, particularly from the United Nations, the Security Council, the United States of America, the Russian Federation, the Muslim states and the European Union.

——— • ◆ • ———

# ISRAEL'S RESPONSE TO THE ROADMAP, MAY 25, 2003

1.   Both at the commencement of and during the process, and as a condition to its continuance, calm will be maintained. The Palestinians will dismantle the existing security organizations and implement security reforms during the course of which new organizations will be formed and act to combat terror, violence and incitement (incitement must cease immediately and the Palestinian Authority must educate for peace). These organizations will engage in genuine prevention of terror and violence through arrests, interrogations, prevention and the enforcement of the legal groundwork for investigations, prosecution and punishment. In the first phase of the plan and as a condition for progress to the second phase, the Palestinians will complete the dismantling of terrorist organizations (Hamas, Islamic Jihad, the Popular Front, the Democratic Front Al-Aqsa

Brigades and other apparatuses) and their infrastructure, collection of all illegal weapons and their transfer to a third party for the sake of being removed from the area and destroyed, cessation of weapons smuggling and weapons production inside the Palestinian Authority, activation of the full prevention apparatus and cessation of incitement. There will be no progress to the second phase without the fulfillment of all above-mentioned conditions relating to the war against terror. The security plans to be implemented are the Tenet and Zinni plans. (As in the other mutual frameworks, the Roadmap will not state that Israel must cease violence and incitement against the Palestinians.)

2.   Full performance will be a condition for progress between phases and for progress within phases. The first condition for progress will be the complete cessation of terror, violence and incitement. Progress between phases will come only following the full implementation of the preceding phase. Attention will be paid not to timelines, but to performance benchmarks. (Timelines will serve only as reference points.)

3.   The emergence of a new and different leadership in the Palestinian Authority within the framework of governmental reform: The formation of a new leadership constitutes a condition for progress to the second phase of the plan. In this framework, elections will be conducted for the Palestinian Legislative Council following coordination with Israel.

4. The Monitoring mechanism will be under American management. The chief verification activity will concentrate upon the creation of another Palestinian entity and progress in the civil reform process within the Palestinian Authority. Verification will be performed exclusively on a professional basis and per issue (economic, legal, financial) without the existence of a combined or unified mechanism. Substantive decisions will remain in the hands of both parties.

5. The character of the provisional Palestinian state will be determined through negotiations between the Palestinian Authority and Israel. The provisional state will have provisional borders and certain aspects of sovereignty, be fully demilitarized with no military forces, but only with police and internal security forces of limited scope and armaments, be without the authority to undertake defense alliances or military cooperation, and Israeli control over the entry and exit of all persons and cargo, as well as of its air space and electromagnetic spectrum.

6. In connection to both the introductory statements and the final settlement, declared references must be made to Israel's right to exist as a Jewish state and to the waiver of any right of return for Palestinian refugees to the State of Israel.

7. End of the process will lead to the end of all claims and not only the end of the conflict.

8. The future settlement will be reached through

agreement and direct negotiations between the two parties, in accordance with the vision outlined by President Bush in his 24 June address.

9.  There will be no involvement with issues pertaining to the final settlement. Among issues not to be discussed: settlement in Judea, Samaria and Gaza (excluding a settlement freeze and illegal outposts), the status of the Palestinian Authority and its institutions in Jerusalem, and all other matters whose substance relates to the final settlement.

10.  The removal of references other than 242 and 338 (1397, the Saudi Initiative and the Arab Initiative adopted in Beirut). A settlement based upon the Roadmap will be an autonomous settlement that derives its validity therefrom. The only possible reference should be to Resolutions 242 and 338, and then only as an outline for the conduct of future negotiations on a permanent settlement.

11.  Promotion of the reform process in the Palestinian Authority: A transitional Palestinian constitution will be composed, a Palestinian legal infrastructure will be constructed and cooperation with Israel in this field will be renewed. In the economic sphere: International efforts to rehabilitate the Palestinian economy will continue. In the financial sphere: The American-Israeli-Palestinian agreement will be implemented in full as a condition for the continued transfer of tax revenues.

12.  The deployment of IDF forces along the September 2000 lines will be subject to the stipulation of Article 4

(absolute quiet) and will be carried out in keeping with changes to be required by the nature of the new circumstances and needs created thereby. Emphasis will be placed on the division of responsibilities and civilian authority as in September 2000, and not on the position of forces on the ground at that time.

13.    Subject to security conditions, Israel will work to restore Palestinian life to normal: promote the economic situation, cultivation of commercial connections, encouragement and assistance for the activities of recognized humanitarian agencies. No reference will be made to the Bertini Report as a binding source document within the framework of the humanitarian issue.

14.    Arab states will assist the process through the condemnation of terrorist activity. No link will be established between the Palestinian track and other tracks (Syrian-Lebanese).

# *Afterword*

———— •◆• ————

Most of my time in recent years has been devoted to work at The Carter Center, where our major emphasis is on the prevention or eradication of diseases among some of the poorest and neglected people on earth. More newsworthy, and perhaps more controversial, have been some of the negotiations we have conducted to end or prevent crises involving armed conflicts and human rights abuses.

Many of these emergencies have been caused or perpetuated by leaders who were considered to be international outlaws or pariahs, and meeting with them, sometimes working with them, was necessary if the destruction of war and human rights persecution were to be ended or prevented.

The work of the Center has taken us to Addis Ababa, Ethiopia, to negotiate with the Communist dictator Mengistu Haile Mariam, to Liberia to induce warlord Charles Taylor to let democratic elections be held, and to Pyongyang, North Korea, to convince Kim Il Sung to give up his nuclear program in exchange for financial assistance and the prospect of future peaceful relations with the United States.

A few months later, in September 1994, Sam Nunn, Colin

Powell, and I flew to Haiti to induce General Raoul Cédras to leave the country and permit the elected president to return, and in 2002 Rosalynn and I made a visit to Havana so that I could speak directly to the Cuban people about democracy and human rights.

The Center has monitored almost seventy elections, often at the invitation of such people as Manuel Noriega, the Sandinistas, and Hugo Chávez. Three of the most honest, fair, and peaceful of our elections have been in Palestine.

In the course of my life I have done things that have provoked controversy. In some cases, I admit the criticisms may have been justified. Nothing in the past, however, has equaled the outpouring that followed the publication of *Palestine Peace Not Apartheid*.

As a child, I was taught by my father every Sunday about the special status of the Jewish people in the eyes of God, and when I was governor of Georgia, I went with my wife and Jody Powell to the Middle East to learn more about Israel and its mortal threats from Arab neighbors. From the time I was a young submarine officer until I became president, I observed closely the four wars fought in the Holy Land. I visited Yad Vashem three times and wondered why there was not a public commemoration of the Holocaust in America. As president, I inherited a secondary boycott from the Arab members of OPEC against any U.S. corporation that traded with Israel.

In 1977, the Cold War and the danger of nuclear confrontation were looming, and everyone understood that if doomsday ever arrived, it most likely would dawn in the Holy Land. I was determined to resolve these problems when I was inaugurated, but I realized that to achieve peace in the Middle East I would have to be seen as an honest broker by both sides. In that belief, I followed in the footsteps of my six predecessors, three Democrats and three Republicans. Within three weeks, I called for a Palestinian homeland and began to meet with both Israeli and Arab leaders, including Hafez al-Assad and Anwar al-Sadat, both of whom were then considered by many to be villains because of their wars against Israel. The meeting with President Sadat paid rich dividends.

I wrote this book to cover two subjects that are rarely openly talked about in America: the terrible plight of the Palestinians and the need for a balanced discussion of how Israel and her neighbors can find peace and live together with mutual respect.

Well, I certainly got the discussion, and though it has sometimes generated more heat than light, I remain convinced that such a debate is very much in the interest of the people of the Middle East and of the United States.

We are seeing some glimmers of hope, both in the Middle East and in Washington. The Arab nations have, once again, made an offer that has been welcomed by President George W. Bush and other members of the International Quartet and even by Israeli prime minister Ehud Olmert. The proposal promised full peace for Israel with all Arab nations if Israel withdraws to its 1967 borders and a fair solution is found for Palestinian refugees. Secretary of State Condoleezza Rice has stated that this Arab offer is the foundation for her wavering peace effort.

The Arab declaration is a major step in the right direction, although this offer must be modified as prescribed in the Geneva Initiative. This is a precise and definitive peace proposal endorsed by President Clinton, Prime Minister Tony Blair, President Jacques Chirac, and more than fifty other world leaders and approved by a majority of Israelis and Palestinians.

I honor the courage that prevails among Israelis and Palestinians who have been constantly frustrated year after year but have persisted in their search for peace with justice. Nobody enjoys being called ugly names, but what I have experienced is of little importance compared to the half century of suffering, death, persecution, and fear experienced by the people of Israel and Palestine. Many of them have continued to work and sacrifice peacefully and without violence, while opportunities were lost because of shortsighted leaders and extremists on both sides, and by repeated failures of imagination and courage on the part of our own government.

I know these people, in Jerusalem, Gaza, and Ramallah, and they have my sympathy and admiration. Consistently, for three decades, I have seen public opinion polls within Israel that show more than 60 percent of the citizens approving the exchange of Palestinian land for peace, and in January a poll revealed that 81 percent of all Palestinians share this same desire.

With a few exceptions, we have seen the prospects for peace largely decline since the treaty between Israel and Egypt, achieved by the courage of Anwar Sadat and Menachim Begin twenty-eight years ago. Yitzhak Rabin was another hero and, like Sadat, he was assassinated because he was a man of peace.

On both sides, three generations have sacrificed their lives or their freedom in the search for reconciliation. But these courageous people cannot achieve peace and justice by themselves. With the exception of one bold move by Norway in 1993, history has shown that progress is possible only if the United States assumes its historic role of honest broker.

To play that essential role, America must not be seen as "in the pocket" of either side; we must enjoy a degree of trust and respect from both sides. We must always make clear our commitment to the security of Israel, but we cannot be peacemakers if American government leaders are seen as knee-jerk supporters of every action or policy of whatever Israeli government happens to be in power at the moment. That is the essential fact that must be faced.

A powerful factor, especially in the political arena, is the domineering influence of the American Israel Public Affairs Committee (AIPAC), which exercises its legitimate goal of defending the policies of Israel's most conservative governments and arouses maximum support in our country. Under AIPAC pressure, there are few significant countervailing voices in the public arena, and any balanced debate is still practically nonexistent in the U.S. Congress or among presidential hopefuls.

The American friends of Israel who demand such subservience are in many cases sincere and well-intentioned people, but on this crucial issue, they are tragically mistaken. Their demands subvert America's ability to bring to Israelis what they most desperately need and want—peace and security within recognized borders.

As a father, a grandfather, and now a great-grandfather, I cannot help but think especially of the children. A baby born during the first Arab-Israeli conflict will be fifty years old next year. Peace between Israel and her neighbors is also vital to the interests of our own children here in America though for somewhat different reasons. Today the growth of Islamic extremism and the unprecedented hostility toward America in the Islamic world is directly related to the continuing bloodshed between Israelis and Palestinians. To think otherwise is foolish and dangerous.

My prayer on behalf of the children of the Holy Land and America is for the gift of courage to Israeli and Palestinian leaders, but particularly to our elected officials of both parties and at both ends of Pennsylvania Avenue: the courage to face the facts and do what is necessary, to return America to its honored and historic role as a peacemaker.

Jimmy Carter
May 2007

# ACKNOWLEDGMENTS

More than a quarter century ago, I joined Egyptian President Anwar Sadat and Israeli Prime Minister Menachem Begin in signing a peace treaty between their two nations, following four wars since the nation of Israel became a reality. These leaders had committed themselves to justice for the Palestinians, the withdrawal of Israeli military and political forces from the occupied territories, and an opportunity for Israelis and all their neighbors to live in harmony with each other. The parliaments in Cairo and Jerusalem ratified the agreements, which were overwhelmingly approved by the citizens of both countries and have never been violated.

Since then, many of the promises have been broken and there have been constant cycles of bloodshed and a rising tide of mistrust and hatred. This book is designed to examine the root causes of the continuing conflict and to spell out the only clear path to permanent peace and justice in the Holy Land.

Most of my personal involvement in the troubled region since leaving the White House has been as a representative of The Carter Center, an organization that is dedicated to promoting peace, freedom, human rights, and the alleviation of suffering. My associates there have helped me to understand the complex interrelationships within Israel, among the Palestinians, and between them and the neighboring governments. Matthew Hodes, David Carroll, and others have been actively involved in formulating reasonable peace proposals and encouraging democracy. My personal assistants, Faye Perdue and Lauren Gay, have provided good advice in the preparation of my manuscripts, and Dr. Steve Hochman has joined my wife, Rosalynn, in perusing the text to detect and eliminate errors.

At Simon & Schuster, I have had the invaluable assistance of Alice Mayhew as my astute and forceful editor; Serena Jones, her assistant; and Paul Pugliese, who prepared the maps. I also want to express my gratitude to Lynn Nesbit, my agent, who has blessed me by arranging this partnership with such an extraordinary publishing firm.

The University of Arkansas Press has been very gracious in permitting me to use some of the material originally published in my *Blood of Abraham*, which is still in print and will now have an updated chronology and assessment of recent developments in the Middle East.

# INDEX

————— •◆• —————

Page references in *italics* refer to maps.

## *About the Author*

Jimmy Carter was born in Plains, Georgia, and served as thirty-ninth President of the United States. He and his wife, Rosalynn, founded The Carter Center, a nonprofit organization that prevents and resolves conflicts, enhances freedom and democracy, and improves health around the world. He is the author of numerous books, including *An Hour Before Daylight*, called "an American classic," and the #1 *New York Times* bestseller *Our Endangered Values*.

# Also by Jimmy Carter

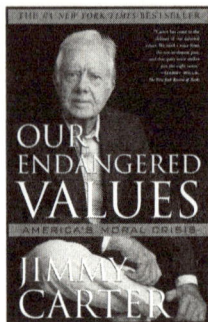

In this #1 *New York Times* bestseller, President Jimmy Carter offers a passionate defense of separation of church and state. He warns that fundamentalists are deliberately blurring the lines between politics and religion.

"Carter has come to the defense of our national values. We need a voice from the not-so-distant past, and this quiet voice strikes just the right notes."—Garry Wills, *The New York Review of Books*

---

Lavishly praised and an instant national bestseller, *The Hornet's Nest* is the former president's dramatic novel of a little-known and important chapter of the Revolutionary War.

"Carter has written an involving, exciting novel about the War for Independence as it was fought in Georgia and the Carolinas, backwaters usually overlooked by Massachu-centric historians." —*The Wall Street Journal*

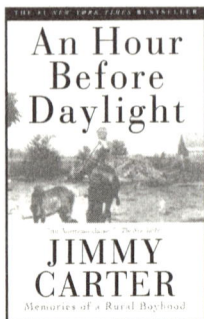

---

In his singular voice and with a novelist's gift for detail, Jimmy Carter creates a sensitive portrait of an era that shaped the nation and recounts a classic American story of enduring importance.

"A lovely and haunting piece of work . . . conveys with quiet passion . . . its author's love for the place in which he grew up and where, he says, he expects to rest for eternity."—Jonathan Yardley, *The Washington Post Book World*

"An American classic."—*The New Yorker*